Catalyst

W9-AED-515

2012-2013
UVa
School of Architecture
University of Virginia

Editor
Ghazal Abbasy-Asbagh
Lecturer in Architecture

Student Editorial team
Rebecca Hora MArch 2013,
Ryan Metcalf MArch 2013,
Matthew Pinyan MArch 2013

Kim Tanzer, Dean
Edward E. Elson Professor of Architecture

Catalysis - the speeding up, or sometimes slowing down, of a chemical reaction by adding a substance which itself is not changed thereby.

Catalyst perfectly captures the energy, passion, and production of this moment in the School of Architecture at the University of Virginia. Focused in the design disciplines but extending to all four of the School's departments—architecture, architectural history, landscape architecture, and urban and environmental planning—*Catalyst* provocatively indexes the work we do while prompting further reflection for those of us charged with shaping the School's trajectory.

Like its etymological cousin, *Catalyst* demonstrates both the speed and the slowness of the School of Architecture's efforts. The sections titled "Crisis" and "Stasis" demonstrate the balance of urgent responses—to social inequities, climate change, toxins, and trash—with constant, consistent responses—manifest in the predictability of material processes and human behaviors. "Flux" frames the flow between these two, found in design projects located across the world and here in Charlottesville.

Catalyst captures the unfolding, to use the physicist David Bohm's term, of the School's efforts through a diverse range of individual faculty and student projects, and its enfolding into one decades-long drive toward a sustainable, just future. As a collective, the School's year-long focus on water—the "After the Deluge" dialogues, the Woltz Symposium titled "Quasi Objects," and the all-School charrette, titled "The Rivanna River Vortex"—catalyzed our shared attention.

Similarly, the tension between speed and slowness is evident in our methods of production, from hand-built projects proposed for MoMA's PS 1 to those in Africa, to parametric cascades of information and speculative form.

In an environment so fertile, modulating the fast and slow, the individual and the collective, the constant and the changing is our singular privilege. We are pleased to present *Catalyst*, which provides a glimpse of the rich creative flux that is the University of Virginia School of Architecture.

On behalf of the School of Architecture I offer my special thanks to Ramon Prat, publisher of Actar Publishers, for his belief in our work; to Iñaki Alday, Quesada Professor and Chair of the Department of Architecture, for making this match with Actar; to Ghazal Abbasy-Asbagh for her careful curation of the School's efforts; and to Rebecca Hora, Ryan Metcalf and Matthew Pinyan for their tireless editorial assistance.

Iñaki Alday, Chair
Department of Architecture, Quesada Professor

Foreword

Catalyst will be the first comprehensive critical compilation of a year of teaching and research within the School of Architecture at the University of Virginia. It documents the work done within and across all departments, work that embodies the overlapping and interconnected relationships which are necessary for any effective action in the contemporary world. Founded almost one hundred years ago, the UVa School of Architecture is one of the oldest and most recognized schools in the country and a leader among public universities. Architecture is the most public of the creative arts, the one capable of generating cities and landscapes, spaces, volumes, and voids. It is the one that portrays, even shapes, societies at each moment and place in history. At UVa, we claim the value of some words intimately linked but often dismissed: design, public, politics.

This is a unique School, one that strives to continually reinvigorate the strong soul outlined by its founder, Thomas Jefferson. From this foundation, the School has developed a deep social and political commitment on the basis of which architecture*—in the broadest sense—serves the construction of a society. The ambition to transform our physical environment and social world through design is shared by every department, faculty member, and student. This common ideal, together with the place and the people, has facilitated what the Italian geographer Giuseppe Dematteis calls a "disciplinary fluidity" that extends far beyond interdisciplinary exchanges among vertical collections of knowledge. The School is a matrix of intertwined and shared expertise bolstered by a collaborative environment in the midst of a competitive world. The School remains profoundly convinced of the contemporary relevance and transformative power of architecture. Disciplinary fluidity and collaboration is a constant throughout both our research and curriculum. Emblematic of this is "The Vortex," the annual all-School workshop and competition, which brings together some three hundred students of all levels and departments to work together full-time for a week with the annual Robertson Visiting Professor (Adriaan Geuze in 2013, Eduardo Arroyo in 2012).

The School's seminars and workshops are open to all throughout the year. This extends to the graduate Research Studios offered by architecture and landscape architecture faculty to the students of any and all departments.

The Research Studios, both in the graduate and undergraduate sequences, make up half of the studio curriculum. In the undergraduate program, after the well-established foundational courses "Lessons in Making" and "Lessons of the Lawn," students take a sequence of three Foundation Studios: "Introduction to Design," "The City," and "Inhabitation." The first introduces architecture and design in the broad sense and scales: structure, construction, urban systems, and living spaces. The second year begins with investigations about the territory and the city and culminates with an urban project that transforms a part of the city. In the spring of the second year, the focus on the space of inhabitation leads to an urban project and the design of housing. City and inhabitation, polis and dwelling place, social space and human shelter—all in nonlinear sequences with strong graphic and theory components—make up the foundation of the design curriculum. Similarly, the graduate programs of architecture and landscape architecture start together in the Summer Design Institute (SDI) and continue in separate Foundation Studios until merging again in the Research Studios.

The Research Studios, the elective seminars, and the independent thesis give the most accurate portrait of the uniqueness of the various programs. The rotating research topics are offered consistently over several semesters by the faculty and selected strategically by the students, who take control of their own education as designers and citizens. Topics include:

> > **Environmental crisis and extreme conditions.**
> > **Water, rivers, hydrological networks, and natural dynamics as matter of design.**
> > **New urban models, retrofitting the city, the new suburbia, biophilic cities, and healthy environments.**
> > **Material explorations and recycling/upcycling trash as construction resource.**
> > **Social inhabitation, immigration, and cultural and economic development.**
> > **Political crisis and architectural responses.**
> > **Coastal and land occupation under climate change.**

The independent design thesis projects produced this year in the School dive deep into many of these topics, developing sometimes highly specific research such as generative maintenance in landscape, new construction codes for developing countries, or urban planning and building design for incremental population and social change in contemporary India. All these research topics express what the UVa designers and scholars care about, regardless of scales or a priori—and already forgotten—disciplinary boundaries. But this ethical and social activism, a fundamental part of the School's DNA, is expressed through our expertise—in architectural design. And the value of this design work, besides the ethical component, stands by itself under the ruthless scrutiny of aesthetic and formal judgment.

Through the contents of *Catalyst* and its editorial discourse, as well as through our daily work, the School explores the challenges in both the education and practice of architecture today, as well as the social role of architects and architecture. Environmental and social challenges are fundamental elements of our practice and education. To face them, multiple scales and logics must be addressed together and integrated. From the territory and the landscape to infrastructure, the city, the urban project, buildings, public space, and microarchitecture, no one scale is disconnected from the rest, even those on the opposite side of the spectrum. Similarly, a variety of topics, often in conflict with one another, are intertwined, creating new conditions and new questions that drive new ideas and responses. Technologies, materials, systems of production—the core of tectonic knowledge—are all part of these conditions and opportunities for innovation.

In many places and situations, the current challenge for architecture is to retain, even recover, its relevance to society. The UVa School of Architecture's abiding commitment to the social centrality of architecture, arising from its inescapably public nature, means that we cannot ignore this challenge.

We recognize that the role of the architect and the discipline of architecture are at a critical juncture and seize that as an opportunity. Architecture's social and ethical function finds its form in the creative management of complexity, in opening up to a wider and wider range of topics and activities, and in awareness of its political and social impact. The creative process cannot be secluded or isolated. Architecture transforms the physical environment synthetically and comprehensively, embracing all the diverse kinds of expertise necessary for an expanded design practice. This is true for both conventional building projects and emerging hybrid programs at any scale.

Architecture is technical but also ideological and cultural; it defines the purposes and strategies of each transformation of our environment. Architecture involves both change and permanence; it materializes, shapes, and articulates the values of our time and place; and it participates in and is evaluated according to contemporary intellectual discourse and a dynamic understanding of history. The UVa School of Architecture, where scholars and practitioners meet to teach, learn, and research, is the place to face the challenges of the education and the role of architecture in this exciting and defining moment.

*architecture in this text is taken in its broad sense, and refers to the four areas integrated in the School of Architecture at the University of Virginia: architectural history, architecture, landscape architecture, and urban and environmental planning

Ghazal Abbasy-Asbagh, Editor
Lecturer, Department of Architecture

Introduction
The Contemporary Predicament: Conditions and Responses

In his 1939 essay "Avant-garde and Kitsch" Clement Greenberg asks how it is that a culture produces a poem by T. S. Eliot and a poem by Eddie Guest: "What perspective of culture is large enough to enable us to situate them in an enlightened relation to each other?" [1] Nearly seventy-five years later, in the age of Google-mania, Architizer, Archinect, Archdaily, twitter, instagram, and so on, the question of the vanguard—cultural or architectural—is far more convoluted. What we have is a flattening of mass and high culture, in which avant-garde and kitsch are no longer diametrically opposed: "In a kind of Warholian dream, every echo has become an original artwork." [2]

This edited volume gathers a range of formats, project types, scales, and representation styles within the framework of various disciplinary processes, research agendas, and pedagogical approaches, under the rubric of one institution. In curating this work, we have presumed the interest and commitment of the academy to the production of knowledge and to innovation, hence the interest of this introductory text in a definition of "avant-garde" within which the work of the UVa School of Architecture can situate itself.

Greenberg's question therefore remains relevant, and to answer it requires moving beyond aesthetics and examining the relationship between individual experience and its historical and social contexts. It is important to acknowledge that the conditions of our contemporary reality—the flattening of mass and high culture—make this a particularly complex and challenging task.

The work collected here is examined based on the premise that our contemporary moment—within which UVa School of Architecture operates—is largely defined by two interrelated and intertwined factors:

one is the realization that our current modes of existence are no longer ecologically, economically, or socially sustainable; the other, the hypermediatization of this reality, which produces an intensified awareness of this condition in popular and intellectual imagination.

While this moment of crisis parallels several others in our recent history, it is this intensification that distinguishes our current historical moment.
In response to this, the process of curating this volume can be understood as an attempt to position oneself with respect to environmental conditions—social, economic, and ecological. This position in turn necessitates a rethinking of the avant-garde and perhaps a break with the inward-looking academicism that dominated some forty years of architectural discourse.

This volume, therefore, purports to be a litmus test to measure whether environmental conditions—sociopolitical or ecological, notwithstanding their cultural, technological, and disciplinary contexts—are catalysts for new modes of practice and pedagogy. To this end, the contents are organized in three states or conditions:

crisis, stasis, and flux

At a moment overwhelmed by the staggering quantities of information—images and data—made available to us by the World Wide Web and its many nets, the task of a collection such as this goes well beyond documenting the moment, framing future projections, or even the potential of re-branding or re-imaging a School. The cyclical nature of the academic setting demands short-term projects, which remain unresolved and are judged in only a few minutes by a panel of experts.[3] These exercises, however, become the seed of an interest in the topics and approaches that are at the core of design pedagogy. The work in this volume was curated with an eye to cultivating that interest. When curating the work of some two hundred authors one has to be judicious and cautious—at all times aware of all two hundred entries in relation to each other. What became abundantly clear after a few rounds of reviews is that the thread that tied all the work together was a decided investment in responding to the forces that shape our contemporary reality. Following this thread, the questions we asked were:

What is the impact of design on the forces that shape our contemporary reality?

To what extent do contingencies of time and place shape our response?

How does the discursive nature of design education contribute to this feedback loop?

Our intention is not to produce a conclusive answer to any of these questions, but rather to suggest that the discipline has devised many modes and methods for responding, some of which provided the secondary categorization of the work included here, listed as "responses":

type, prototype, systems, generative details, paradigm shift

The responses have been generated by way of crowdsourcing the work within existing frameworks and do not claim to offer a comprehensive narrative, nor a scientific categorization of contemporary methods of design practice.

This binary—conditions and responses—has allowed us to speculate on how our mode of operation shifts in the face of the environmental conditions we confront. As the work is organized in three chapters—the three states or conditions, crisis, stasis, flux—the categorization starts to loosely suggest tendencies in the disciplinary responses that comprise the secondary layer of organization. In response to ecologies and landscapes that are in a constant state of flux, systems that have the capacity to be scalable, transformable, and dynamic become the prevalent way of working. As crisis exposes the fault lines of our current state, utopias and grand narratives are intent on producing a paradigm shift. Whereas stable conditions have allowed for moving forward disciplinary research in materiality, tectonics, spatial structures, and working typologically. In this way, the volume has become a means by which the work of the School could be related to the environmental design disciplines at large.

To answer the questions that we have posed, it is necessary to inquire into the position of the avant-garde(s)—in plural if possible—with respect to the history of the discipline and its modes of operation. Greenberg's definition of avant-garde emphasized a distancing or detachment from existing paradigms, at a moment when a culture became stale and stagnant. When "creative activity dwindles to virtuosity in the small details of form," that is the moment in which the avant-garde is born, articulating itself in contradistinction to a reified status quo. In architecture, this clearly marks early modernism as an avant-garde moment, which produced a language entirely its own in response to novel sociopolitical, technical, and cultural conditions. Modernism as the point of departure has remained the frame within which we have operated, whether we've opposed it or embraced it. Perhaps Lavin best addresses the link between modernism and our contemporary moment: "Over the past several decades, Modernism has been rejected, superseded, repeated, deformed, preserved and supersized, remaining by virtue of these very occlusions the most active frame through which every contemporary is identified." [4]

As revealed in the makeup of several panels of distinguished speakers at a conference held at MoMA in 1996 on this very topic, it is uncanny that most presenters—theorists and practitioners—situated the avant-garde within an extended history of the discipline, tracing it back to the early modernist visionaries.[5] While the notion of a historical avant-garde has come to be widely accepted in architecture, the temporal incongruity of this notion indicates the paradoxical character of an avant-garde that exists in time. Although students are exposed to a good deal of the discipline's extended history, with a decided focus on early modernism as the seed of our current modus operandi, inevitably the frame of reference has shifted towards a great many other topics, at the fore of which are environmental exigencies. he impact of the handful of required and elective history and theory courses, considered alongside the ubiquitous news feed or rss feed or a variety of other feeds is dwarfed, if not entirely negligible.

A cursory look at the idea of a historical avant-garde reveals that it may partially originate in the discourse of "autonomy" which, Reinhold Martin suggests, was largely the product of Eisenman's effort to give primacy to architecture in the face of the growing environmental and communication trends of the late '60s and early '70s. Martin refers to a series of articles published by Eisenman from 1970-73 in which he formulated a theory of environment in sharp contrast to those attempted at the time by Banham (in *The Architecture of the Well-Tempered Environment* or *Los Angeles: The Architecture of Four Ecologies*) and Ian McHarg (in *Design with Nature*). These articles were an attempt to "retrieve a ground for architecture ... as a defensive measure undertaken to defer absorption into the media-ecological spectacle ... pointing architecture inward rather than outward." [6] In 1970, President Nixon signed the National Environmental Policy Act (NEPA), which declared the 1970s as the decade that "America pays its debt to the past by reclaiming the purity of its air, its waters and our living environment." This was followed by a thirty-seven-point antipollution program that noted, "as we deepen our understanding of complex ecological processes ... much more will be possible." Needless to say, this collapse of the "national and supranational" environment and the common goal of environmental protection, as elaborated in the decree, were not necessarily self-evident in the wake of the Vietnam War and the use of napalm. What the decree did, however, was to contribute to an already changing perception of the "environment," from an immediate and proximate "socio-biological milieu" to a complex ecological and economical network, hence providing the framework for a shift in popular and intellectual imagination.[7]

While the questions of the autonomy and agency of architecture have produced some of the most invigorating discourse in the discipline, the question now, forty years later, at yet another moment of crisis is: what is the discourse? Is the discipline in need of salvation again? Or should it be allowed to slip down the slippery slope of the growing environmental apparatus?

If we do allow for the avant-garde to be situated outside this historical paradigm, where would we place it? The early definitions of the avant-garde included an antibourgeois attitude, which by default had sociopolitical connotations, as uninterested as the early "settlers of Bohemia" may have been in politics.[8]

At a moment well beyond the optimism of the boom era [9] and its often toxic relationship with the environment, fully immersed in the plethora of environmental crises and operating within increasingly grim economic conditions, today's avant-garde–distancing itself from the formalism that was fed by the mechanisms of the boom era—is similarly implicated in politics.

The revolutionary attitude[10] of the '60s and early '70s has given way to environmental activism, but there is very little about the environment that does not involve policy and politics. In fact environmental activism has brought about a whole new social order, one that ties our politics to our diet and has generated a whole new financial regime. What this says about the sundering of avant-garde and politics is beyond the scope of this introductory text, but what is certain is that this has never been a clean break. This is perhaps most evident specifically in the planning discipline, where larger-scale operations involving many players impact large segments of society. The work of Suzanne Moomaw in the communities of the Virginia coalfields (Sp13) is one that tries to build on bottom-up processes and community-based activism, in order to make incremental change and undo the impacts of policies that have for decades ignored the environmental, ecological, and health implications of such large-scale operations.

Building on technological advances, network theory, and cybernetics, these processes have in fact infiltrated the social sciences as well as environmental design practices, resulting in a "paradigm shift," defined by Kuhn as the reconstruction of the field from new fundamentals, a reconstruction that changes some of the field's most elementary theoretical generalizations as well as many of its methods and applications.[11] In architecture and landscape architecture specifically, these processes have produced the idea of "field conditions," or "bottom-up phenomena, defined not by overarching geometrical schemas but by intricate local connections." [12]

This "reconstruction from fundamentals" is precisely the working method of studios and seminars taught by Phinney ("Parametric Fiction," Sp13 & "Soft Surfaces," Fa12) and Dripps ("Future Fit," Fa12), which build on contemporary technologies to incorporate methods and processes outside conventional practice. "Future Fit" investigates possible overlaps of "gradient spatial networks" with urban infrastructures, posing the question of whether "infrastructures can be emergent, responsive, self-regulating, and inherently self-sustaining?" In doing so, it speculates on the possibility of urban schemas being generated vis-à-vis "connectivity and social aggregation," rather than conventional top-down processes.

flux / systems

Building on bottom-up processes where a specific detail, node, or component becomes a starting point, "Surface FX" (Osborn Fa12), "Planted Form and Function" (Gali Sp13), and "On the Rivanna River" (Gali Sp13) respond to emergent conditions of ecologies and landscapes that are in a constant state of flux by producing scalable, transformable systems. In "WASH," Aja Bulla-Richards (MLA'13) investigates the possibility of transforming monofunctional infrastructures to "resilient socioecological systems." In "BIM Unplugged" Suau (MArch'13) builds a catalogue of methods and processes that close the gap between the construction methods of the West and their implementation in developing countries. In response to the emergent conditions of the American mill town—specifically Danville, VA—the studios and theses directed by Menefee ("Void Operations," Fa12 and Sp13) test out "combinations of entrepreneurial and practical thinking—spatial and economic" that would generate systems for sustainable urban conditions. These projects produce systems and ecologies that would otherwise be outside the scope of the design discipline's formal tendencies.

crisis / utopia

Having considered the end of the historical avant-garde, one cannot help but ponder the fact that each era, each generation, sees itself at the cusp of a new paradigm and predicts the end of another. If the early twentieth century saw the production of a new cultural paradigm, which in architecture translated to a desire to undo the Beaux-Arts in so many ways, the mid-twentieth century saw the end of the very same cultural wave. In his seminal 1984 essay on postmodernism Fredric Jameson observed: "The last few years have been marked by an inverted millennarianism, in which premonitions of the future, catastrophic or redemptive, have been replaced by senses of the end of this or that, the end of ideology, art, or social class; the 'crisis' of Leninism, social democracy, or the welfare state, etc. etc." [14] For Jameson, this constituted what came to be known as postmodernism, the existence of which, he speculated, depended on "the hypothesis of some radical break or coupure, generally traced back to the end of the 1950s and the early 1960s." Ever since the "end of modernism" we have also witnessed the end of history (Fukuyama, 1992), the end of theory in architecture (as argued by Lavin), the end of utopia (1992), the end of the world (1995), "The End of the Classical – The End of the Beginning, The End of the End," [15] and "After all, or the End of 'The End of.'" [16] This "break"—the end of modernism—produced yet another trend, catapulted by the political and social events of the '60s and '70s. The utopias of this era became the foundational steps of a "paradigm shift," one that would be pursued again, at yet another moment of crisis. Visions of utopia have historically escalated in the presence of undesirable sociopolitical and economic conditions, and generally tend to reinvent the current conditions and often do so in a pseudo-scientific manner, using part science, part fiction. In recent years, catastrophe, pollution, shortage, excess—in short, **crisis**—have become a platform for innovation. "The Rivanna River Vortex," "Future Fit" (Dripps Fa12), "Parametric Fiction" (Phinney Sp13), "End of the World" (Jull Fa12), "paradox city" (Hugo BSArch'13), "War zone" (Pinyan MArch'13), and "Tokyo 2050" (Iizuka MArch'13) all produce utopian visions and grand narratives that imagine unprecedented conceptions of the environment. While these visions clearly build on the provocative megaprojects and paper architecture of Super Studio, Archigram, and Archizoom, among others, their approach produces systems and ecologies that arguably surpass the questions of formal autonomy and historical form. Although many of these projects remain pseudo-scientific provocations, in an exceedingly global world where information can be accessed, disseminated, and archived almost instantly without geographic boundaries, it is possible to imagine that their approach might make a mark on the landscape of a rapidly urbanizing world.

Further rehashing the question of the impact of early modernism's revolutionary ideas, still the source of much debate and unrest, manifests the role of these ideas in giving rise and legitimacy to such popular trends as New Urbanism and its many offshoots and knock offs—perhaps also a coupure, but with different ambitions—which is precisely what the "Suburbia" studio (Alday Fa12) responds to: "Suburban growth in the past decade has produced an impossible and unrecognizable 'popular' style which entails the erasure of landscapes and the application of standard solutions, which are rather related to a funny combination of Disney and *The Simpsons* than to any urban, landscape, or architectural thought." Sheila Crane's seminar, "Transnational Modernisms," takes on this issue by considering "discrepant histories of modernity." By mapping "transfers of materials, objects, architects and architectural knowledge across national, geographical, and cultural boundaries" it investigates alternative critical framework for modern architecture, a methodology that could be widely applicable to our contemporary modes of practice as well.

stasis / type

It is precisely the rapidly changing environment that foregrounds the role of environmental design disciplines in stabilizing these conditions. Responding to this need, working **typologically**, studios taught by Clark ("A Place to Live and Work" Fa12 and "Community and Privacy" Sp13), Dripps and Abbasy ("Monster" Sp13) have focused on housing. Housing, as the **dominant type** in the city, mediates between the public and private realms. "Monster" considers emergent conditions—social, ecological, and economic—as platforms for producing new cultural hybridities. Whereas in "A Place to Live and Work," W.G.

Clark starts with the condition of the site as a **stabilizing** factor in addressing the condition of dwelling—one that allows the vision of a balance between dwelling and working. Likewise, "Design Specificity" (Crisman Fa12) builds on emergent cultural paradigms to test the rigor of the public institution and its relationship to the city. Waldman ("A Culinary Institute" Sp13) produces spatial experiments in response to highly nuanced programmatic require-ments, placed in a site and a city of the student's choosing. The freedom in choosing a city foregrounds the role of the city as protagonist in shaping the spatial structure of this typology.

Embedded in a great public institution, with strong political and social tendencies, the School has found its calling in responding to desolate land-scapes, natural catastrophes, financial crisis—in short, the wicked problems of the world. [17] The interdisciplinarity of its approach emerges out of necessity in response to the complex conditions of our historical conjuncture. Due to its geographic location—a peripheral space almost entirely free from many of the constraints that have shaped the discipline and left their footprints on its discursive landscape—the School has maintained an experimental approach. "Away from the center, you're at the edge. The power of looking from the edge is the ability to discover weakness and possibilities at the center. A strength of this place has been its ability to capitalize on this." [18]

**This has provided the School with a mode of operation defined by strategic interventions at a perceived edge, one that can never be understood outside its fraught relationship to the (admittedly fictive) center.
This peripheral position arguably provides the working grounds for a mode of operation that is less interested in "detaching itself" as the early avant-garde purported to do, but one that is more invested in strategic interventions.**

The research the faculty pursues, often conceived of as small initiatives such as ecoMOD and reCOVER, among many others, has generated broad platforms that operate simultaneously in multiple domains and within hybrid disciplines. Prompted by the growing ecological and economic crisis, the role of architects, landscape architects, and planners as stabilizers is in fact reasserted because of our ability to cast a wider net, which enables a level of exchange between the far corners of the world, rendering the world a global village, on which programs like the India Initiative and the China program build.

The optimism, can-do attitude, and do-it-yourself ethos of the current generation, and their willingness to tackle issues well beyond conventional scopes have redefined "avant-garde" as optimistic, opportunistic, pragmatic, and strategic.

Notes

1_Clement Greenberg, "Avant-Garde and Kitsch," *Partisan Review* 6, no. 5, (1939), 34.

2_Mark Wigley, "Network Fever," *Grey Room* 04 (Summer 2001): 114.

3_Student editors Rebecca Hora and Matthew Pinyan reflect on this in *Catalyst* (2013): "Much of the work produced in a school of architecture has a short lifespan: pinned up for a brief moment, critiqued, documented, and consequently packed away. This work is often viewed as a series of discrete individual projects completed by students, suspended in a specific moment in time and framed by its immediate audience. The true power of a school's work, however, lies in its identity when viewed as a whole—as a clear statement of values evidenced through a series of explorations, experiments, and research efforts. Paper Matters exists to pursue this agenda: to give the UVA School of Architecture a platform by which to exchange and make known the values of our faculty and students" (203).

4_Sylvia Lavin, "Buildings, Texts and Contexts," Harvard Graduate School of Design, Fall 2007.

5_Greg Lynn, "In the Wake of the Avant-Garde," *Assemblage*, 29 (April 1996): 116-25.

6_See Reinhold Martin, "Environment c. 1973," (*Grey Room* 14 [Winter 2004]: 78-101) for an extensive discourse on Eisenman's approach, via Chomsky's idea of "deep structure" in linguistics.

7_Ulrich Beck,Risk Society: *Toward a New Modernity*, trans. Mark Ritter (London: Sage Publications, 1992).

8_"In seeking to go beyond Alexandrianism, a part of Western bourgeois society has produced something unheard of heretofore: – avant-garde culture. A superior consciousness of history – more precisely, the appearance of a new kind of criticism of society, an historical criticism – made this possible... New perspectives of this kind, becoming a part of the advanced intellectual conscience of the fifth and sixth decades of the nineteenth century, soon were absorbed by artists and poets, even if unconsciously for the most part. It was no accident, therefore, that the birth of the avant-garde coincided chronologically – and geographically, too – with the first bold development of scientific revolutionary thought in Europe. True, the first settlers of bohemia – which was then identical with the avantgarde – turned out soon to be demonstratively uninterested in politics. Nevertheless, without the circulation of revolutionary ideas in the air about them, they would never have been able to isolate their concept of the "bourgeois" in order to define what they were not." Greenberg, "Avant-Garde and Kitsch," 35.

9_The economic boom of '90s and early '00s produced "starchitecture" that enjoyed unprecedented artistic freedom, budget, and size. .

10_Mary McLeod reflects on the effects of this period on architecture education in the US: "Although many of the institutional and pedagogical changes in design education remained, including a somewhat less hierarchical teaching environment and a larger focus on urban and social issues, most of the more radical experiments in learning came to a halt once the original student activists graduated." "The end of innocence: From political activism to Post modernism," in *Architecture School: Three Centuries of Educating Architects in North America*, ed. Joan Ockman (Cambridge, MA: MIT Press, 2012), 164.

11_Thomas S. Kuhn, *The Structure of Scientific Revolutions* (Chicago: University of Chicago Press, 1962).

12_Stan Allen, *Points + Lines* (New York: Princeton Architectural Press, 1999), 92.

13_Fredric Jameson, "Postmodernism, or the Cultural Logic of Late Capitalism," *New Left Review* 146 (July-August 1984): 59.

14_In her introductory essay in a recent issue of the Journal of Architectural Education, Christina Contandriopoulos compares the narratives that "stressed the end" to those that gave way to the "narratives of after," speculating on their impact on the return of utopia in the twenty-first century. "Architecture and Utopia in the 21st-Century," *Journal of Architecture Education* 67, no. 1 (2013): 3-6.

15_Peter Eisenman, "The End of the Classical: The End of the Beginning, The End of the End," *Perspecta* 21 (1984): 154-173.

16_K. Michael Hays and Alicia Kennedy, "After All, or the End of 'The End of,'" *Assemblage*, 41 (April 2000): 6-7.

17_In their 1973 essay "Dilemmas in a General Theory of Planning" (*Policy Sciences* 4 [1973]: 155-69), Horst W. J. Rittel and Melvin M. Webber contrast the "wicked problems of the world" from the "tame problems of the world," arguing science does not have solutions for the former.

18_Robin Dripps, "Jefferson's Legacy, NOW," *Catalyst* (2013).

Catalyst

CONDITIONS / RESPONSES

199 Flux

Catalyst

CONDITIONS / RESPONSES

Crisis

At a moment well beyond the optimism of the boom era and its often toxic relationship with the environment, fully immersed in the plethora of environmental crises and operating within an increasingly grim economic outlook, new experimental approaches have emerged that build on current technologies and the overlaps of multiple disciplines. These experiments pursue a more holistic and systematic approach to engaging the environment. Crisis becomes a platform for innovation.

What are some of the mechanisms that could reverse the damages caused by industrialization on natural resources such as rivers? (Crisis 17)
Can large scale centralized infrastructures be reconceived as human-scale networks that are adaptable and scalable? (Crisis 33)
How can ground-up initiatives challenge conventional practices? How do the realities of budgets, construction schedules and the real estate market impact these initiatives? (Crisis 55)
How can architecture act when confronted with changes whose scale exceeds human control? (Crisis 73)
Can infrastructure be emergent, responsive, self-regulating, and inherently self-sustaining? (Crisis 85)

After the Deluge

Symposia: A Demonstration of the Practical
Imagination Applied to the Ecology of Water

Dialogues:
Reimagining Leonardo's Legacy,
The Rising,
The Contaminated,
The Disappearing

In the fifteenth century, Leonard da Vinci fused an artist's persuasive understanding of water with an engineer's reasoned response in his "Deluge" series of drawings and his proposal to contain the flooded Arno River. Since that time, science has moved to the center of human discourse while art and visualization have often been relegated to the realm of the merely illustrative, decorative, or entertaining. But persistent catch phrases such as "a picture is worth a thousand words" and "the heart has reasons that reason knows not of" serve to remind us that art, too, is a persuasive form of logic.

This demonstration of the practical imagination—an exhibition and four dialogues—is inspired by Leonardo's synthetic approach to problem solving. The subject of the demonstration, water and the varied ways it epitomizes the challenges of environmental sustainability, was chosen because water is ubiquitous on the blue planet, and research and creative work on the subject is widespread across the University of Virginia, and the greater Academy. "After the Deluge" was held during the Spring 2013 semester. Hosted by the School of Architecture, it incorporated artists and scientists from across Grounds who were paired with nationally recognized artists or scientists.

Kim Tanzer

"After the Deluge" was part of a year-long School-wide focus on the subject of water. For the larger effort, see "drink" at http://www.arch.virginia.edu/resources/all-school-research-focus-water

Reimagining Leonardo's Legacy; presenter: Leslie Geddes
Map of the Arno River, 1502-04 (Royal Library, Windsor Castle)

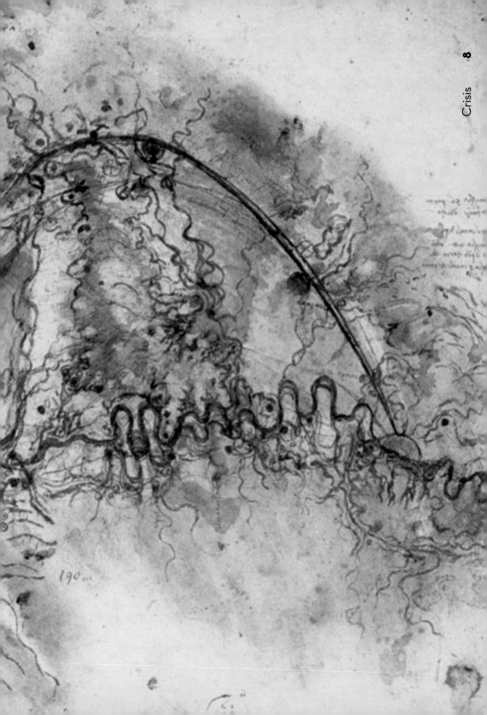

Dialogue 1: Reimagining Leonardo's Legacy

On Leonardo da Vinci's fascination with flows—water, clouds, and other natural processes

Keynote   Leslie Geddes, Ph.D. candidate, Princeton University
Panel   Matthew Reidenbach, Dept. of Environmental Science
            Hossein Haj-Hariri, Professor and Chair, Dept. of Aeronautic and Mechanical Engineering
            Francesca Fiorani, Dept. of Art History
            Nana Last, Dept. of Architecture
Moderator   Kim Tanzer, School of Architecture

Dialogue 2: The Rising

On flood circumstances, particularly related to climate change

Keynote   Matthew Burtner, Dept. of Music, Composition, and Computer Technologies, UVa
Panel   Matthew Jull and Leena Cho, School of Architecture
            Iñaki Alday, Elwood R. Quesada Professor of Architecture and Chair, Dept. of Architecture
            Pat Wiberg, Dept. of Environmental Science
Moderator   Kim Tanzer, School of Architecture

Dialogue 3: The Contaminated

On waters compromised by human actions

Keynote   Brandon Ballengèe, Ph.D. candidate, University of Plymouth, artist, and biologist
Panel   Phoebe Crisman, Dept. of Architecture, Director of Global Sustainability program
            Jim Smith, Dept. of Civil Engineering
            Rebecca Dillingham, Director, Center for Global Health
Moderator   Kim Tanzer, School of Architecture

Dialogue 4: The Disappearing

On water shortages and drought

Keynote   Margaret Ross Tolbert, artist and environmentalist
Panel   Brian Richter, The Nature Conservancy
            Paolo D'Odorico, Dept. of Environmental Science
            Janet Herman, Dept. of Environmental Science
Moderator   Kim Tanzer, School of Architecture

AQUIFERious Virginia

Margaret Ross Tolbert

Paintings, multimedia art, and excerpts from the book *Aquiferious* by Margaret Ross Tolbert, winner of the Florida Book Award 2011

Dean's Gallery, School of Architecture, February-May 2013

Gallery Talk March 29, 6:00pm

Reimagining Leonardo's Legacy; presenter: Leslie Geddes
Map of the Arno River, 1502-04 (Royal Library, Windsor Castle)

The Rising; presenter: Iñaki Alday
Secondary dike failure, Mississippi, 2011

The Contaminated; presenter: Brandon Ballengèe
2010 Deepwater Horizon oil spill in the Gulf of Mexico

The Disappearing; presenter: Janet Herman

Margaret Ross Tolbert
AQUIFERious Virginia

On Practical Imagination

Francis Bacon, the seventeenth-century philosopher, divided knowledge into three parts: Memory, Reason, and Imagination. Thomas Jefferson, following Bacon's work, divided his own library into three sections which he titled History, Philosophy, and Fine Arts. Jefferson's library formed the foundation for the Library of Congress.

Due to the persuasive power of Bacon's work, and that of his contemporary René Descartes, much of the intellectual effort of the last three hundred years has been devoted to the pursuit of reason. Known as the Age of Enlightenment, this period gave rise to the scientific method and the

development in the nineteenth century of the modern concept of science and the role of the scientist. At the heart of the Enlightenment project is a search for the cause of that which exists. Left to atrophy in this quest for certainty has been the important role of imagination—that which might exist. Indeed, the fine arts, including architecture and oratory, along with theater, painting, dance, and music, seem only to be appreciated by connoisseurs. This proposal seeks to resuscitate the important third branch of Bacon's and Jefferson's organization of the world's knowledge through the creation of a curriculum in practical imagination.

The limits of scientific thinking are evident all around us. Causality and replicability, two hallmarks of the scientific method, help us understand existing circumstances. Such circumstances can be predictive only if the conditions that led to them can be repeated. As systems theory teaches us, in practice this is possible only within bounded experiments or time- or scale-limited real-life events. Heraclitus said several millennia ago, "You could not step into the same river, for other waters are ever flowing on to you." Science,

The Okagavango River does not reach the ocean: it ends with an inland delta in the Kalahari. From *The Disasppearing* Dialogue, presented by Paolo D'Odorico, source: Space-shuttle photograph, Johnson Space Center

DFA 23, Khárôn 2001/07
From *The Contaminated* dialogue,
Peter Ballengee

"While imagination is often viewed as impractical, the practical is too often unimaginative. The practical imagination seeks to celebrate this paradox and, in so doing, find a way to move past the regrettable dichotomy that often splits art from science, leaving both impoverished." Kim Tanzer

by definition, has only a limited capacity to envision alternative futures, or to conceive of multifaceted casuality.

While the scientific method has led to great advances in our understanding of and ability to impact the world, it is time to rekindle the active and rigorous pursuit of the imagination.

Imagination can be generally defined as (1) the act or power of forming a mental image of something not present to the senses or never before wholly perceived in reality; (2) creative ability, the ability to confront and deal with a problem, the thinking or active mind; or (3) a creation of the mind or a fanciful or empty assumption. In current times, imagination is too often aligned with the third definition and dismissed as a fanciful or empty assumption. In the same way, the fine arts, using Jefferson's term for this category of knowledge, are often disparaged as luxuries created to satisfy a small group of cultural elites. But the first definition, suggesting the ability to envision the future, or to make connections between unlikely things, holds underexplored promise. It is this use of the term "imagination" that suggests new avenues for interdisciplinary teaching and research at the University of Virginia. The phrase "practical imagination" is a catachresis, or purposefully mixed metaphor. It conflates the improbability, beauty, and inspiration found in the arts with the dutiful resolve necessary for doing the world's work. While imagination is often viewed as impractical, the practical is too often unimaginative. The practical imagination seeks to celebrate this paradox and, in so doing, to find a way to move past the regrettable dichotomy that often splits art from science, leaving both impoverished. At the same time it celebrates Jefferson's emphasis on useful knowledge.

"As an architect, I think that what we do is incredibly important but not always widely understood. Every chance I have to make connections and to show off the great work that is done here helps not just our faculty and our students, but our standing in the University and beyond." Kim Tanzer

Interview with Dean Tanzer

Following the completion of the symposium, Dean Tanzer and the *Catalyst* editors discussed the intentions, successes, and implications of "After the Deluge." Portions of the discussion are included here.

Dean Kim Tanzer (KT)
Catalyst team: Ghazal Abbasy-Asbagh (GA)
Ryan Metcalf (RM), Matthew Pinyan (MP)

MP What we found most interesting about the symposium was that always a panelist from a scientific background paired with someone from a very aesthetic field. We were wondering what you had anticipated coming out of that dialogue and, looking back, what actually came of that dialogue—what was that relationship and how might it affect the trajectory of the School moving forward?

KT Let me start with the connection between art and science. During the Renaissance and thereafter, there seemed to be a growing chasm between what we think of now as art and what we think of now as science, whereas in the late medieval times and early Renaissance, the people who were artists were also scientists—Leonardo is a great example, which is of course why we still call him the Renaissance Man. To me, that has always seemed like a really unfortunate split. My hope was that through this project we could begin reconnecting these two sides of our cultural production—of our civilization's production—at least in our own local world. I was very conscious of having both artists and scientists and people like architects, who I would argue are "in between."

A second part [of your question] was how might [the relationship between art and science] affect the School's work in the future? One of my roles as Dean is to support the work of faculty, to help them grow as scholars and designers, partly because it's important for the reputation of the School and partly because it's important for our students. By inviting artists, scientists, architects, and landscape architects to work together, my goal in part was that our own faculty would make connections they might not otherwise have made and, similarly, that people from across Grounds would have the opportunity to meet our faculty and get to know their work.

As an architect, I think that what we do is incredibly important but not always widely understood. Every chance I have to make connections and to show off the great work that is done here helps not just our faculty and our students, but our standing in the University and beyond. For the faculty, that was a goal; for the students, of course, it was to help them think synthetically across boundaries. The symposium was structured so that each dialogue could be stand-alone or one could participate in all of them. To plan the symposium we had a luncheon at OpenGrounds to which I invited everyone in the School, in addition to forty other faculty members from across Grounds. Really, we crowd-sourced the dialogues. I adopted the theme that Seth McDowell and his group had developed for water—the rising, the contaminated, the disappearing—and said there would be four dialogues. We put those three titles on the board, as well as the introduction on flow and fluidity—the Leonardo idea—and people who came to the luncheon suggested colleagues. It was really a completely collaborative project, aside from the premise, which I came up with.

RM The School has always been focused on this idea of interdisciplinarity. Instead of looking so internally, it seems really interesting to turn it on its head and make it more external by engaging the larger University.

KT If you look at our disciplines in a national or international context, you realize that leading-edge people are developing knowledge in consultation with people outside our disciplines. It is very typical to see a team that includes a landscape architect and an ethnographer or an ecologist or a hydrologist. [The symposium] is just doing this within the University of Virginia context; I hope it's a good model for our students, as well as faculty, to learn from.

RM Would you think that the direction the profession is heading is that architects may become not so specialized in one area but able to generalize and glean information from others?

KT Yes and no, with an important caution. I think architects have always—at least in recent decades—had the tendency to think we can know all things because we're architects. That means that we don't know very much about anything. I think it's very good for us to be connectors, but it's also important that we recognize that there are people who have deep knowledge in certain fields. We can't become a hydrologist in two days, but we can know a hydrologist and invite that person to join our teams. Really, that's the goal. Certainly, one of the things I learned from this experience was that we all have preconceptions about how other disciplines think. If we can come with an open mind to learn from others, it will help us create a better built environment.

That's the kind of interdisciplinary approach I'm hoping we can focus on.

GA What I found really interesting about what you were doing was that you were trying to do this by making connections to art. It is true that we are operating more and more with an interdisciplinary approach, but you chose to draw parallels with art.

KT Yes, because I think that really good artists are very thoughtful, deep thinkers. We can come to know through drawing, as well as through quantitative methods. There was a period in time when this was understood, but with the beginning of the Age of Enlightenment the role of the arts began to atrophy and the role of logic and method became more prominent.

Now there are alot of people who think that the arts are like cake decorating— just frou-frou for people who have money. I think this is profoundly wrong-headed and it is what I hope we can change through these kinds of efforts. The artists we brought in—Matthew Burtner, Brandon Ballengèe, and Margaret Tolbert in particular—are just amazingly smart, thoughtful, rigorous people working within their own methods of production.

MP So what are you thinking of for next year?

KT I'm beginning to think about the role of visualization and imagination as a particular subject.

MP In terms of representation?

KT I'm not sure we'll use the term "representation," but the symposium will have something to do with getting ideas out of our heads and into the physical world.

I've always been interested in the connection between how scientists visualize the world and how architects embody that understanding in space. Scholars argue the connection is consistent up until the 20th century, when science became so abstract that it became hard to encode in space in the same way. We might think about the Renaissance, when the idea that the sun rotated around the earth was echoed in centric plan organizations; or the Baroque period, when astronomers discovered ellipses in the cosmos, and designers started mapping ellipses into urban spaces.. We see these spatial parallels up until the 20th century, but it's really hard to visualize physics today.

The attempts I've studied of the 20th century I haven't found very persuasive; I'm thinking of Cubist architecture for example, or some explorations of chaos theory, which is very provocative as a concept in physics and science, but in my view, less compelling in architecture. Can we use emerging means of visualization to move beyond the Cartesian paradigm?

This is the second edition of an ambitious experiment in an all-school design workshop involving the Departments of Architecture, Landscape Architecture, Urban and Environmental Planning, and Architectural History. As a collaborative and interdisciplinary activity, nearly 360 are involved in thirty vertically structured teams. Each team has a cross-representation of all generations and all departments evenly and randomly distributed. Water—which connects much of the School's work across all four disciplines and all six research themes—is the subject of the workshop. The focus of the workshop is the Rivanna River corridor in Charlottesville—specifically beginning with Meadow Creek and extending downstream to Moore's Creek —understood not as a barrier but as a potential connector between Woolen Mills and Pantops. The Rivanna River serves both to collect much of the region's storm-water runoff and, until now, to draw a boundary between the two communities along with their political entities, the City of Charlottesville and Albemarle County. Much of Charlottesville's water supply is also taken from the Rivanna River upstream.

Charlottesville, Virginia
Crisis
Paradigm Shift

With a watershed of hundreds of square miles the Rivanna River is a community resource of vital importance to the entire region of Central Virginia across its forty-two mile run. So the workshop emphasizes the fact that local actions have broader consequences, reaching ultimately to the James River and onward to the Chesapeake Bay.

In an immediate sense, the Rivanna is both a boundary and a shared asset. Drawing in Pen and Darden Towe Parks brings the design potentials to include trails and transportation alternatives. At the other end, Moore's Creek is in desperate need of remediation for pollution, sediments, and biological health. The Rivanna Conservation Society and the James River Association plan to focus on Moore's Creek in the next year.

In a run of the river that totals about three miles, diverse and inventive design solutions are needed to connect, remediate, sustain, preserve, and activate the populations and ecologies. The City of Charlottesville is especially interested in investigating issues of design and development as they relate to our hydrology at multiple scales; from the vantage point of our regional watershed to local district-wide drainage patterns to the street, block, and parcel level. Ultimately the results of the investigation will be used to inform the creation of local policies and plans that promote high-quality urban form and public places while safeguarding river health both at the neighborhood

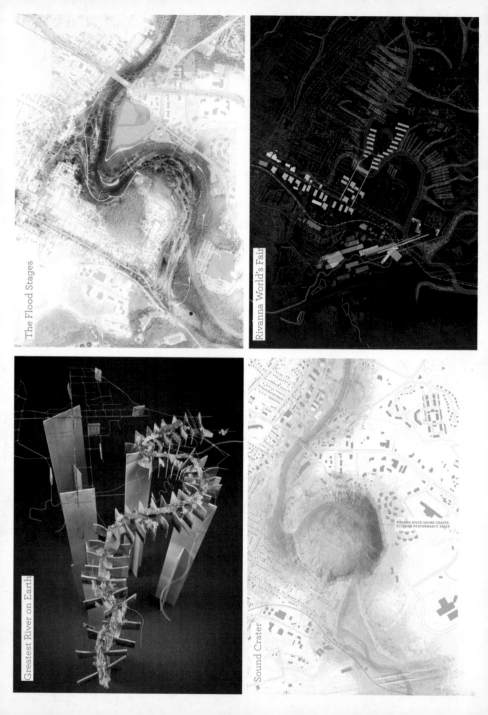

The Flood Stages

Rivanna World's Fair

Greatest River on Earth

Sound Crater

RIVANNA RIVER SOUND CRATER
OUTDOOR PERFORMANCE SPACE

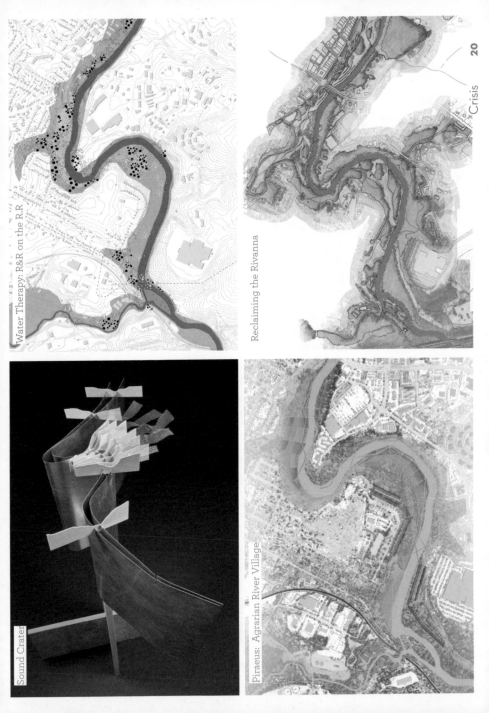

Water Therapy: R&R on the R.R

Sound Crater

Reclaiming the Rivanna

Piraeus: Agrarian River Village

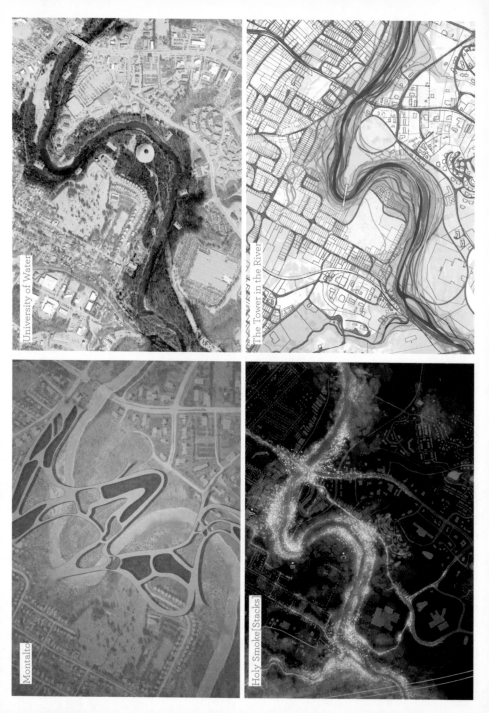

Montalto

University of Water

Holy Smoke (Stacks)

The Tower in the River

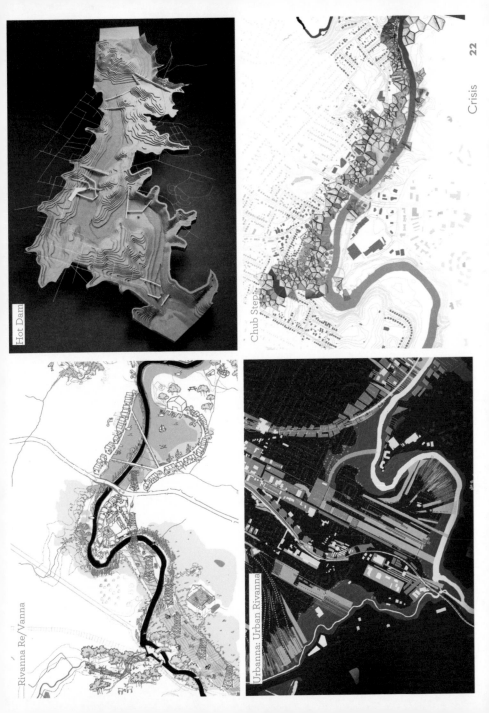

Hot Dam

Chub Step

Rivanna Re/Vanna

Urbanna: Urban Rivanna

Recalibrating the River

Rebalancing Social and Political Dynamics through Water Infrastructure

Erin Root, MLA 2013, M.Arch 2011_Thesis
Advisors: Leena Cho, Teresa Gali-Izard,
Anselmo Canfora, Bill Sherman

In the interest of catalyzing a broader conversation around alternatives to large-scale damming, this thesis reconsiders how water is collected and stored for human and agricultural use in villages in the arid region of Limpopo, South Africa. The design aims to rescale water infrastructure from large centralized constructions to human-scale networks, and to shift this infrastructure from a fixed to a more flexible, adaptable system. This design strategy emphasizes the traditional role of water as a shaper of public space. Women in Limpopo spend one-third of their lives collecting water. This time includes not only that spent at the community spigot and the river's edge, but also the significant time it takes to walk to these sources. Both destination and path are public domains in constant flux. The destination and the route are to be considered in the redesign of this critical infrastructure. This strategy comprises a set of tools that is adaptable to the landscape and the needs of the community. As opposed to the top-down construction of megadams, this design would be implemented and maintained by the community, giving them independent and autonomous control of their water source.

Limpopo, South Africa
Crisis
System

MULENZHE

upstream [above-grade] downstream

waste

store

use

move

extract

upstream downstream

Pesticides and Nitrates

Coliform Bacteria and Ecoli

rural areas use only 3.5 % of the water supply in the limpopo river basin

of residents in rural communities use the municipal tap as a primary source

agriculture uses 50.5% of the water supply in the limpopo river basin

rural communities use surface water as a secondary source

spend 1/3 of their lives collecting and transporting water

from boreholes are only turned on 68.4% of the time

Controlling and culverting water is a global epidemic. By implementing large-scale, fixed, siteless water infrastructure we are changing our relationship to water and its role in the landscape. By burying and pumping water directly into homes we are privatizing a resource that was once central to public space. By damming rivers and piping water to specific places for specific populations, we are commodifying this resource and subjecting one of our most basic needs to social and political dynamics. In addition to its social impacts, large-scale damming negatively affects our ecological systems. An alternative strategy is needed—an infrastructure that takes into consideration seasonal rainfall, human and agricultural needs, and existing ecological flows.

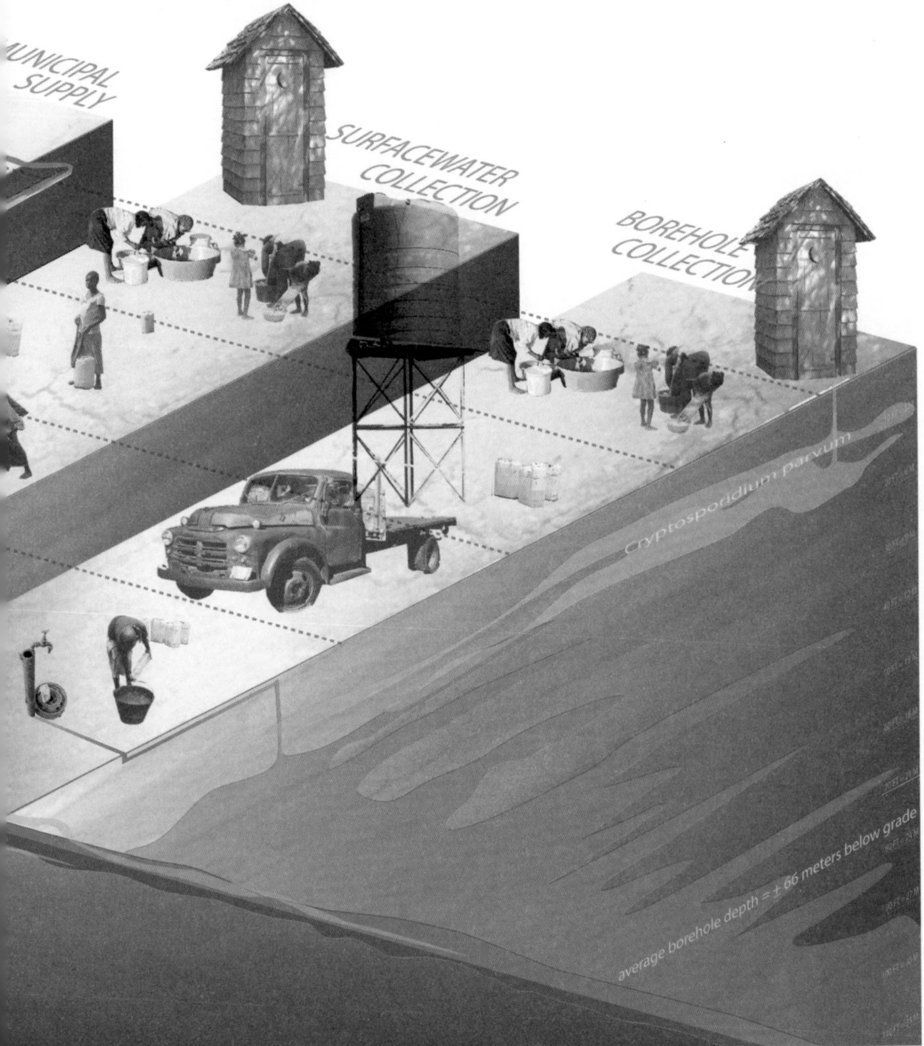

MUNICIPAL SUPPLY

SURFACEWATER COLLECTION

BOREHOLE COLLECTION

Cryptosporidium parvum

average borehole depth = ± 66 meters below grade

A River + a Road

**Rethinking Civic Infrastructure along the Jones Falls Corridor
in Downtown Baltimore
Jorg Sieweke_Spring 2013_Foundation Studio**

How did we arrive at a hostile divide in the middle of the city? *What would the
river do* to bring it to life again? How will the Jones Falls Corridor best serve
Baltimore and the Bay in the future? The central, synthetic character of the
bundled infrastructure corridor indicates a culmination of all critical urban
conditions in Baltimore.

Site/System   The Jones Falls represents a spatial sequence from a steep valley
of urban wilderness lined with early industrial mills to a bundled traffic infrastructure corridor on the floodplain, running into the former delta of the Inner
Harbor area. The linear infrastructure of railway and motorway weave across the
river until the Jones Falls River is buried into an underground concrete conduit
just west of Penn Station. The subway-sized culvert opening is where the river
"ends" and this studio project begins.

History   The Jones Falls River once shaped the valley and created a delta in
the Inner Harbor. The river provided fresh water and energy and served as the
natural infrastructure to found the young emerging city. With Jonestown—the
first settlement on the east bank—regulation of the river began. Severe flooding
washed out the early settlements. In the process of modernization the river was
first walled and finally submerged and degraded as a sewer to make room for
an expressway. In the age of mass motorization (1960s) the roads were scaled
to an expressway. Protest at the time prevented the construction of a cloverleaf
over today's Inner Harbor and left the interstate traffic dispersed into the urban
fabric. Traffic studies suggest that the existing grid of roads could compensate
for the conduit condition.

Baltimore, Maryland
Crisis
System

Whose right of way? The monofunctional conduit of the Jones Fall corridor favoring the suburban motorist commuting to a downtown workplace represents suburban flight and urban blight poured in concrete. The engineered and buried river occasionally reemerges from its underground condition. Storm water floods parts of the highway and the adjacent districts, and hurricanes occasionally push water from the Bay up into the former delta area. How can the boundary/barrier condition be transformed into an adaptive system that serves multiple social and ecological aspects of a contemporary urban lifestyle? How can the hybrid, multifaceted condition of the river be reintroduced?

Potential Several initiatives suggested razing the expressway and turning the corridor into an urban boulevard that would then spur mixed-use urban development of underutilized adjacent property, help raise taxes, and enhance the urban vitality of the disadvantaged neighborhoods. This studio explores the potential for reconsidering the relationship of the given infrastructure elements within the Jones Falls corridor. How can the conduit concept of flows be reestablished in its multifunctional character of gathering and distribution? How can the corridor as a former multipurpose front yard that turned into a backyard be reevaluated to prevent it from becoming the junkyard of the city?

Post-neoliberal city? What are the criteria for urban public infrastructure today that will spur urban life, place making, and redevelopment? What infrastructural system provides adequate service for the next phase of modernization? What investment and regulations need to be developed to stop the down-cycling of the adjacent neighborhoods? Is there a proactive strategy that would anticipate future adaptations? Can strategic asset management in civic infrastructure and the public sphere help to reduce public spending on social services and healthcare?

First we shape the river—then it shapes us!

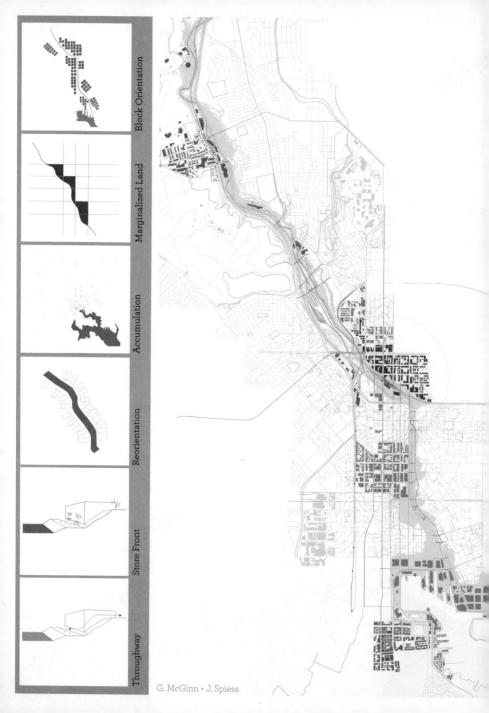

Block Orientation

Marginalized Land

Accumulation

Reorientation

Store Front

Throughway

G. McGinn + J. Spiess

This project investigates the reactivation of the river corridor through accumulation on the topographic edge that divides the upper urban fabric from the lower river corridor. This space is a point of tactical insertion to promote the accumulation of people, water, and culture. Like an eddy in a river these points can serve as a place to slow down and build interaction.

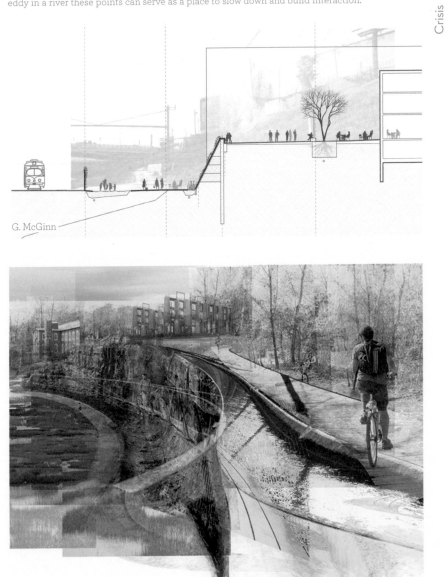

G. McGinn

J. Spiess

"The modernist notion that new physical structures would yield new patterns of socialization has exhausted its run, failing by virtue of trying to contain the dynamic multiplicity of urban processes within a fixed, rigid, spatial frame that neither derived from nor redirected any of the processes moving through it. This emphasis on urban processes is not meant to exclude spatial form but rather seeks to construct a dialectical understanding of how it relates to the processes that flow through, manifest, and sustain it ... the ability to shift scales, to locate urban fabrics in their regional and biotic contexts, and to design relationships between dynamic urban processes and urban form.

Dynamic relationships and agencies of process become highlighted in ecological thinking, accounting for a particular spatial form as merely a provisional state of matter, on its way to becoming something else. Consequently, apparently incoherent or complex conditions that one might initially mistake as random or chaotic can, in fact, be shown to be highly structured entities that comprise a particular set of geometrical and spatial orders. In this sense, cities and infrastructures are just as "ecological" as forests and rivers."

(Corner, *The Landscape Urbanism Reader*, 2006)

WASH

Urban Hydrological Networks for Resilient Cultural Ecologies

Aja Bulla-Richards, MLA 2013, M.Arch 2011_Thesis
Advisors: Brian Osborn and Bill Sherman [2013],
Bill Sherman and Jorg Sieweke [2011]

This project proposes prototypical interventions that reconfigure stormwater and greywater infrastructure in order to initiate layered social and ecological structures in a typical Los Angeles neighborhood. Prototypes are proposed at multiple scales, ranging from the individual experience of site amenities to collective policies that define Los Angeles County water networks. Interventions are designed to impact regional scales as well, including the Colorado River watershed. This project utilizes the potential of greywater not only to reduce unsustainable dependence on water importation and its environmental consequences but also to transform monofunctional infrastructure into multifunctional community watersheds. Integrating ecological performance into the fabric of a neighborhood is critical to redefining urban water infrastructure in relation to everyday experience and for questioning the divide between nature and culture.

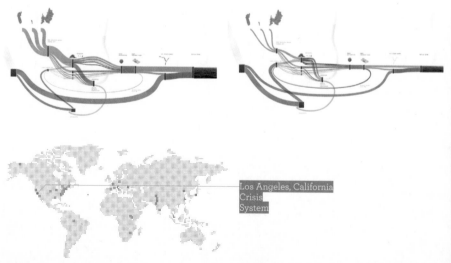

Los Angeles, California
Crisis
System

Arid cities in the western United States are facing an imminent cultural, political, and ecological challenge: dwindling sources of freshwater and a warming climate coupled with rapid population growth. How can we reimagine and redesign water infrastructures so that monofunctional systems can be transformed into resilient socioecological cycles that engage and expand everyday experience, promote alternative cultural practices, and reveal latent ecological processes?

Managing Change, Mobilizing Community

Nate Burgess, MLA 2013_Thesis
Advisors: Brian Osborn, Jorg Sieweke

What alternatives exist besides rigid protection and abandonment that can destabilize entrenched visions of the future and allow barrier island communities to adapt to sea-level rise? What novel economic, social, and ecological proposals are embedded within hybrid retreat strategies, the middle ground between protection and abandonment of barrier islands? This project explores this question through the development of a designed retreat strategy for Sandbridge Beach, VA.

Neighborhood Pier
and Landing

Modular Home
Construction

Wetland Construction

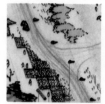

Overwash Road
Construction

Cottage Raising and
Movement

Opting out of the System

Paradox City and the River

Victor Hugo de Souza Azevedo, BSArch 2013_Thesis
Advisor: Nana Last

This thesis is a critique and a response to the urban renewal developments
in the Amazonian city of Manaus, Brazil. It aims to institute a model of
development that keeps the existing social networks intact by inserting
infrastructure and new programmatic elements into informal settlements
while also granting the formal city access to the river, which has long been
neglected. This is a model that is sensitive to the environment and proposes
to work with the population in place. The ultimate goal of this project is to
develop a model that will catalyze gradual social and economic growth in the
river-edge informal settlements.

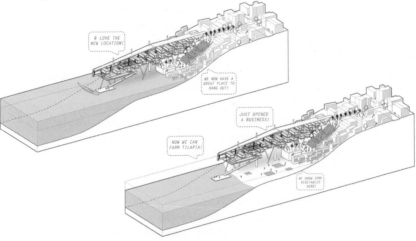

War Zone:
A New Confrontational Ground

Matthew Pinyan, M.Arch 2013_Thesis
Advisor: Iñaki Alday

The twentieth and twenty-first centuries have witnessed a dramatic rise in global conflict and warfare between various countries, political ideologies, and cultural and ethnic groups. Humans have responded to the widespread destruction and loss of life from these events by rapidly constructing physical memorials as symbols and increasingly nationalistic representations of the legacies of these conflicts—victory, loss, grief, remorse.

How might architecture respond to the globalized nature of contemporary conflict? If memorial construction once signaled the end of a conflict, could a new institution emerge as an active participant in the resolution of global warfare? This thesis proposes such an institution, a new city built for confrontation—a space for mediation and resolution of international conflict. Physically separated from the jurisdiction of countries and their governments, this new typology would place (or displace) representatives from opposing sides of a conflict in a completely destabilized environment—the ocean—returning all to the most basic human condition of occupation. Diplomats would occupy this new island during negotiations, the resolution of conflicts spurred by a constant barrage of physical reminders of the costs of war as well as a constantly changing and precarious relationship with the sea.

This new confrontational zone is a mobile warrior, responding to multiple cultures and conflicts over the course of its lifetime.

[siteless]
Crisis
Paradigm Shift

War Zone addresses confrontation not only in the meeting of warring peoples but also in the existence of a constructed, self-sustaining environment within an uncertain, isolated site.

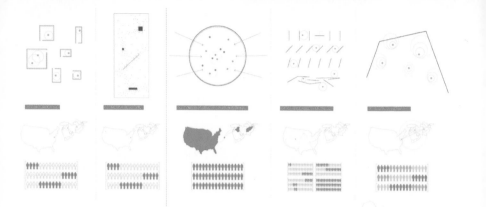

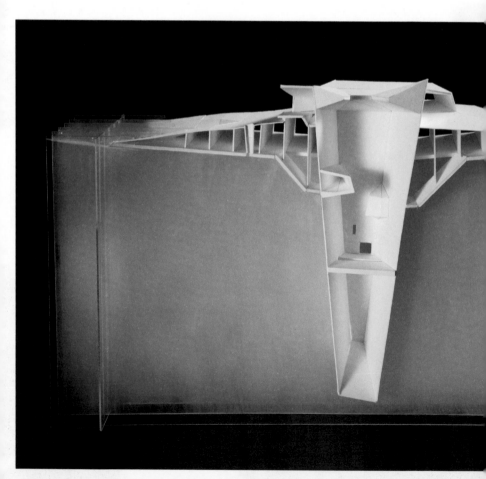

Catalogue of existing
memorial typologies
and speculations on new
architectural responses to war,
specifically a new institution
for confrontation.

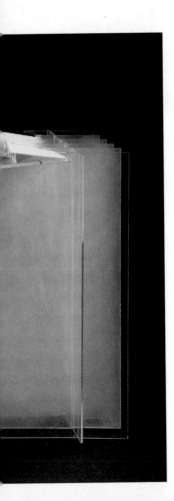

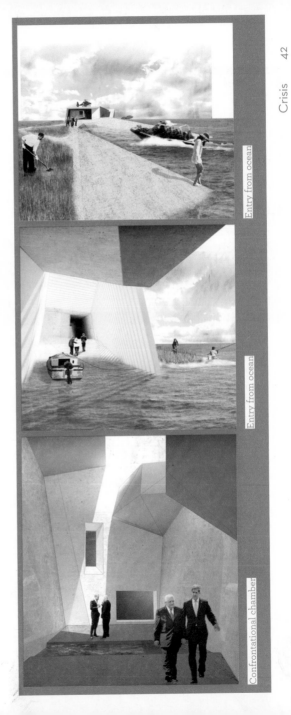

Entry from ocean

Entry from ocean

Confrontational chamber

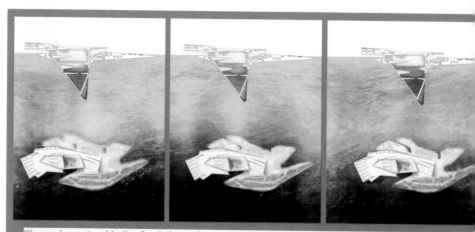

The confrontational hull is flooded over the course of negotiations, changing the building's relationship to the sea and making certain spaces unoccupiable.

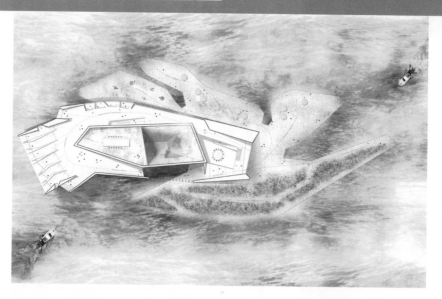

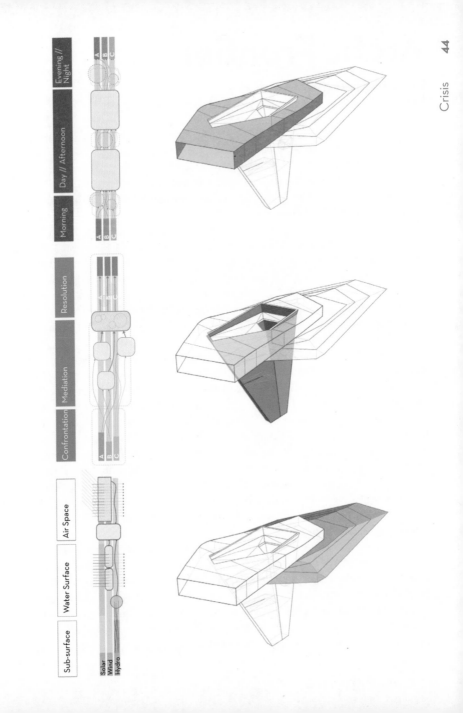

Arctic Frontier

Leena Cho_Spring 2013_Seminar
Katie Jenkins, MLA 2013 + Parker Sutton, M.Arch 2013

Our perception of the Arctic is distorted by biases of graphic and narrative representation. In assessing the Arctic's future, we need a new visual framework. The Flemish cartographer Gerardus Mercator rendered the first complete representation of the Arctic in the sixteenth century. His map depicts four cardinal rivers at the Arctic pole converging on a "bare rock in the midst of the sea ... almost 33 French miles ... all of magnetic stone," where the world's water "descends into the earth ... as if through a filter." It is not this map that Mercator is remembered for, however. The "Mercator Projection" (MP) of 1569 became the standard map for nautical purposes thereafter. Its portrayal of the Arctic was, and is, ubiquitous. Then, as today, this projection describes an Arctic that is dislocated and disconnected. Looking forward, Mercator's original map regains significance. If we understand the Arctic as central, rather than peripheral, we begin to question our inherited perceptions of what lies above the Arctic Circle.

Amundsen, Cook, Hudson, Baffin: Arctic travel has long been associated with stalwart explorers, myths of craggy, glaciated landscapes, and the quest for sovereign pride. For over four hundred years, a sea route through the Arctic has been sought without success: the costs too high and the risks too great. Today, the Arctic is warming at a rate twice that of the rest of the earth. For the first time, straits, passages, inlets, and islands once bound by land-fast ice are navigable. With access to a nearly ice-free Northwest Passage, the shipping industry may soon reduce by a third its 12,600-mile route from Asia to Europe by way of the Panama Canal. Small Arctic towns like Barrow, Alaska, Prudhoe Bay, Alaska, and Iqaluit, Nunavut, are swelling with the arrival of migrant workers imported by oil and gas companies eager to capitalize on thawing ground and retreating ice.

On land, a warmer atmosphere is predicted to push the permafrost's edge northward over three hundred miles by 2100 (Arctic Biodiversity Trends, 2010). In addition to the transformation and eventual loss of much of this unique ground and its coincident habitat, the thawing of permafrost releases carbon dioxide and methane stored within frozen soil, compounding the warming process. Entire ecosystems will migrate north. Once-frozen ground could even become arable land, replacing vestiges of lost agriculture further south.

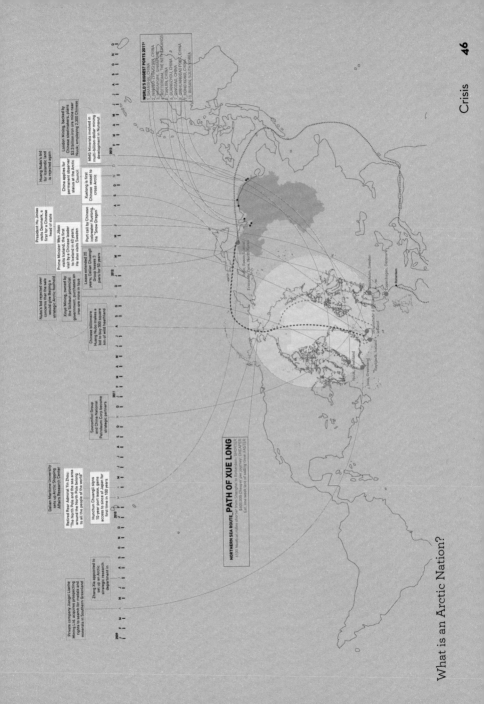

What is an Arctic Nation?

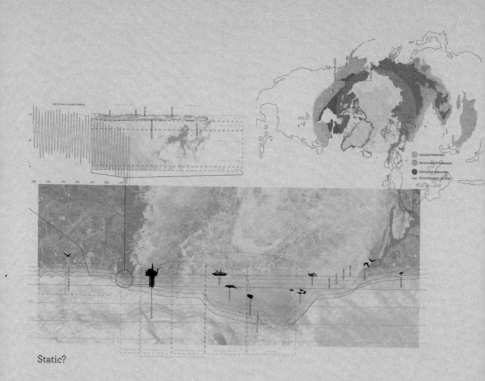

Static?

We are broaching the era of Arctic globalization. As sociopolitical and geophysical forces converge on the Arctic, a terrain that has long been perceived as remote and static becomes central and critical to our everyday life. Designing within the currents of this rapid and monumental change demands that we reevaluate how we read, frame, and represent the Arctic.

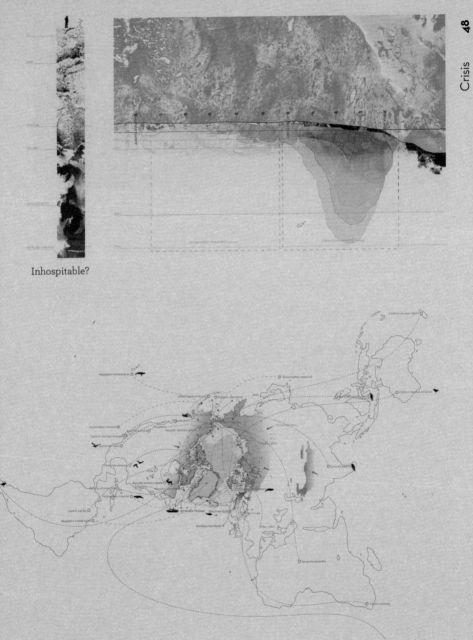

Inhospitable?

Remote?

Addressing Homelessness on Public Right of Way

PI: **Ellen Bassett**, Co-PI: **Andree Tremoulet**, Portland State University
Summary of Research Project by Ellen Bassett_Dept. of Urban and
Environmental Planning

Homelessness is a widespread societal problem in the United States.
The National Alliance to End Homelessness estimates that 636,071 persons
were homeless in January 2011, of whom 243,701 were "unsheltered," meaning
they lived on the streets or in other places not intended for human habitation
(National Alliance to End Homelessness, 2012).
Many of the homeless are transitionally homeless—that is, they are temporarily without a place to stay due to a number of shorter-term factors (for
example, job loss or divorce). But an estimated 17 percent of the homeless
population is considered to be chronically homeless—they are either in and
out of homelessness on a frequent basis or they experience homelessness as
a long-term condition. The chronically homeless are typically the public face
of homelessness. The causes of chronic homelessness are often more challenging than transitional homelessness and include conditions such as physical or mental disability (National Alliance to End Homelessness, 2012).
For many Americans, our main encounters with the homeless take place while
in a car—seeing panhandlers at highway exit and entrance ramps, encounter-
ing people moving with their household effects along the side of the road, or
maybe even spotting homeless individuals sheltering under bridges and over-
passes. It shouldn't be surprising then that the issue of how to manage homeless populations living on transportation land known as the public right-of-
way presents significant challenges for state and local level transportation
agencies. In a survey conducted in the spring of 2012 that had respondents
from twenty-five US states and one Canadian province, we learned that 70

percent of state agencies reported that they had encountered homeless encampments and 40 percent of them considered homeless encampments
to be "an operational challenge."
When asked what kinds of problems the homeless pose for the agency, the
most frequent responses were health/sanitation and safety, including fire,
drugs or needles, and damage to property. Respondents also cited trash and
debris, panhandling, fighting, vandalism, impacts on restrooms, and unattend-
ed children and pets.
So what are state agencies doing to address the issue of homelessness on
public rights-of-way? Our research showed that states tend initially to rely
upon law enforcement—calling in state troopers or local law enforcement
to clear out homeless individuals and their possessions. Such an approach,
however, only serves to shift the problem elsewhere and does not really address the underlying issues—such as the need for social services and access
to affordable shelter. A law-enforcement-only approach also contributes to
adversarial relationships, setting the homeless against law enforcement and
transportation agency personnel, as well as pitting legal aid agencies and
homeless advocates against local governments, transportation agencies,
and law enforcement.
Our research uncovered some notable best practices. The most effective
approaches combine the stick of law enforcement with the carrot of social
services. In the relocation of homeless individuals living in the Baldock Rest
Area in Wilsonville, Oregon, for instance, county social service agencies and
a faith-based area nonprofit worked together to provide case-management
services to Baldock residents. With funding from the state-level housing
agency, the services provided included helping individuals to get their au-
tomobiles repaired, gain access to transitional housing, and enter into drug
rehabilitation programs.

For architects, landscape architects, planners,
and engineers, a critical question is how
to create public spaces and structures that
accommodate the needs of the unsheltered
in order to make being homeless a less brutal
and demeaning experience.

Law enforcement personnel worked to change the administrative rules around rest areas—a weak point in the law previously—to ensure that camping or remaining in the rest area for more than twelve hours was an enforceable violation. Law enforcement also worked with social services to ensure that the final clearance of the rest area was carried out in an orderly and humane manner.

Effective approaches to managing the homeless on public rights-of-way, moreover, are highly collaborative—they draw from the talents and experience of all professionals involved. To work, however, these approaches require a high degree of trust—both between the collaborating professionals and between the homeless communities and the professionals/ agencies working on addressing the specific problem at hand.

Our best practices guide identifies a problem-solving approach that can be adopted when public agency personnel encounter the issue of homelessness. Initially, it is important to understand the parameters of the problem you are responding to: Is it a case of acute endangerment? That is, if unresolved could public safety be at risk? From interviews we learned that a number of states have faced such problems—like encampments on the edge of a busy highway that might endanger both motorists and the homeless themselves. Or is the problem more a simmering nuisance? That is, the homeless may be a persistent presence but not a cause for immediate concern. Often these cases come to the fore when there is a precipitating event such as a complaint from a resident or a business. These two different scenarios require different responses and have different timelines for the actors involved.

We identified three prototype strategies for managing homeless populations on public rights-of-way. The first, humane displacement, has the goal of assisting people at the site to find better living options and to return the site to its original use. The Baldock example referred to above is a case study for this approach; we also highlight work from the Massachusetts Department of Transportation in metropolitan Boston. The second strategy is called short-term accommodation. In this case the goal is more to reduce wear and tear on an existing site in the short term and help the homeless locate a more permanent solution to their housing needs within a set time frame.

An example of this is the early history of Dignity Village in Portland, Oregon. The final strategy is long-term arrangements in which the goal is to accommodate longer-term habitation on a designated site in a way that minimizes adverse environmental and social impacts.

Successful long-term arrangements usually establish strong democratic self-management institutions for residents. Tent City 4 in the greater Seattle area is an example of a long-term arrangement, as is Opportunity Village in Eugene, Oregon. There is a need for more research on this topic. From a public policy perspective, we need to know more about the scope of the problem across different states; we need to develop action plans and evaluate policies for managing the problem. For architects, landscape architects, planners, and engineers, a critical question is how to create public spaces and structures that accommodate the needs of the unsheltered in order to make being homeless a less brutal and demeaning experience.

As one astute traffic engineer commented on our research at the National Transportation Research Board conference, "Why don't we design bridges that are multipurpose? Homelessness is a problem that isn't going to go away—and innovative design should be one of the solutions."

But an estimated 17 percent of the homeless population is considered to be chronically homeless—they are either in and out of homelessness on a frequent basis or they experience homelessness as a long-term condition. The chronically homeless are typically the public face of homelessness.

For project documents including the Baldock Case Study and the Planning and Best Practices Guide, see: http://www.otrec.us/research/researcher/bassett/
Bibliography: National Alliance to End Homelessness. State of Homelessness 2012. http://www.endhomelessness.org/content/article/detail/4362. Accessed July 20, 2012.

"Mass production in architecture, focused chiefly on mass housing, permitted architecture to be seen in a new light. Repeatability was desirable, as it was constant with industry. 'The same constructions for the same requirements,' Bruno Taut wrote, and now the word 'same' needed to be understood *ad litteram.* Industry required repetition, series: the new architecture could be pre-cast. Now the word type—in its primary and original sense of permitting the exact reproduction of a model—was transformed from an abstraction to a reality in architecture, by virtue of industry; type had become prototype."

(Rafael Moneo, "On Typology," 1978)

ecoMOD
ecoREMOD

High Performance Affordable Housing for Charlottesville and South Boston, Virginia

John Quale_Associate Professor and ecoMOD / ecoREMOD Project Director

Paxton Marshall_Professor and ecoMOD / ecoREMOD Engineering Director

Nancy Takahashi_Chair, Landscape Architecture and ecoMOD / ecoREMOD Landscape Advisor

Eric Field_Insight Lab Director and ecoMOD/ecoREMOD Digital Simulation Advisor

Michael Britt_Project Manager and Research Assistant, MArch '12

Elizabeth Jennings Rivard, BSArch '11 **+ Erik de los Reyes**, BSArch '11,

Beth Bailey, MLA '11_Research Assistants

Since 2004, the ecoMOD Project at UVA has worked with a variety of affordable housing organizations to create energy efficient and low-environmental-impact prefabricated housing units. The project includes students and faculty from a variety of disciplines, and collectively they have designed, built, and evaluated twelve housing units on eight sites. In 2007 ecoMOD began to work on renovation projects as well, and in 2009 officially launched a sister project, ecoREMOD.

Charlottesville, Virginia;
South Boston, Virginia
Crisis
Prototype/Type

- The median income for a family of four in Charlottesville is $45,110, and almost 26 percent of Charlottesville residents are below the poverty line (roughly $21,000 in this area).
- Median income for a family of four in South Boston, VA, is $34,848, with 25 percent of residents below the poverty line.
- The average American household spends approximately $2,200 a year on energy. For American families in the bottom quarter of income levels, energy expenditures alone can use up more than 20 percent of their income.

In the Fall of 2012, the ecoMOD / ecoREMOD studio focused on three activities:

ecoREMOD SoBo

an apartment complex rehab with Southside Outreach, South Boston, VA

The team developed a design for a major energy retrofit of a set of 1970s multifamily, two-story apartment buildings that once served as Section 8 public housing and currently provide nonsubsidized affordable housing. Southside Outreach, a nonprofit organization, purchased the dilapidated apartment buildings, and the studio's design has allowed Southside Outreach to visualize the renovation and help them raise funding to complete the project.

ecoMOD Ranch

a prefab system for single family homes with Southside Outreach, South Boston, VA

This partnership has evolved out of the ecoMOD South project. The fall 2012 studio designed an even lower-cost prefab system than ecoMOD South called ecoMOD Ranch. The students generated a set of modules that can be configured in a variety of ways, and preliminary estimates reveal the units can be delivered at the target cost per square foot. If Southside Outreach and UVA are able to bring together enough grant funding, the project will go into construction in the middle of 2014.

ecoREMOD BxB

a block-by-block rehab project with Albemarle Housing Improvement Program (AHIP), Charlottesville, VA

In this multiyear, multi-unit effort in the 10th and Page neighborhood in Charlottesville, students assisted AHIP with assessing a number of homes, and created renovation design solutions that increase energy efficiency. This neighborhood includes a number of late nineteenth- and early twentieth-century single-family detached homes, and has long been one of the city's low-income communities. ecoREMOD AHIP is attempting to touch a large number of buildings in a two-block area in a short time.

The collaborative team in the studio consisted of fifteen graduate and undergraduate students in the studio, a graduate planning student, several graduate and undergraduate engineering students, and two graduate landscape architecture students.

The fabrication process started at the Cardinal Homes manufacturing facility, where the UVA team and Cardinal collaborated over many months on construction details and material selection to achieve Passive House standard.

ecoMOD South
Passive House standard homes in South Boston, VA, and Abingdon, VA

In the summer of 2011, the ecoMOD Project received a substantial grant to commercialize one of the previous ecoMOD designs with a modular homebuilder in Southside Virginia. The grant brought together ecoMOD with Cardinal Homes, and two affordable housing organizations, Southside Outreach in South Boston, VA, and People Inc. in Abingdon, VA. The goal was to create a truly low-cost and high-performance version of the ecoMOD4 design, which had been completed in 2009 for Habitat for Humanity. The design team, which included research assistants that were recent graduates of the School and had previous experience with ecoMOD, elected to target the Passive House standard. In the summer of 2013, the homes were completed—two of them at Passive House standard, and one of them built to the standard building code as a control house. They will all be occupied, and their performance and comfort will be carefully monitored.

reCOVER

Anselmo Canfora_2007-2013

Initiative reCOVER was founded in 2007 to contribute to public-interest architecture and bring together academic, civic, and professional humanitarian organizations to work collaboratively to benefit the common good. Partnerships with organizations assisting marginalized communities to rebuild are an essential part of the work of reCOVER. Helping make tangible the connections between the impact of local interventions and global humanitarian awareness, reCOVER directly involves architecture and engineering students in applied research and real world experiences as an important part of their education and internationally engaged scholarship. reCOVER creates new knowledge in the area of building design and construction while underscoring the importance of proving design concepts through field applications and sustainable practices. Based on a fundamental philosophy that design processes and building methods are interdependent, a building is not simply considered a result, outcome, or even a product of design, but instead is promoted as a collaborative solution well informed by thoughtful research, substantive exchanges, and direct community involvement.

St. Marc, Haiti
Gita + Maiyla, Uganda
Mashamba, South Africa
Crisis
Prototype/Type

Breathe House; St. Marc, Haiti

Primary Schools in Uganda

In partnership with the US-based international nonprofit Building Tomorrow, Inc., the School of Engineering and Applied Science program Engineering in Context, and the Arup Cause program based in the UK, reCOVER is developing a design for a primary school to be built in the Central Region of Uganda. The new primary school design will benefit a group of approximately three hundred children in the village of Maiyla as well as future schools to be built by Building Tomorrow over the next four years. Defined as a translational research project, the central tenet of reCOVER is to develop a prototypical building and landscape design that can be applied as part of a long-term, holistic strategy to improve primary education in Uganda. This is the second such project. The first project was designed by reCOVER for the village of Gita, Uganda, in 2008 with construction completed August of 2010.

Gita primary school, 2009, project manager Jeff Ponitz (M.Arch '08). A second school is slated for construction fall 2013; project manager: Megan Suau (M.Arch '13)

Production and Educational Community Facilities in South Africa

The reCOVER proposal for the Water and Health in Limpopo project focuses on the development of a replicable building system for a ceramic water filter factory, community center, and productive landscape design. Funded by the Jefferson Public Citizens program and in partnership with the University of Virginia's Center for Global Health; the University of Venda in Thohoyandou, South Africa; the Mukondeni Pottery Cooperative; PureMadi; and the Arup Cause Program, the reCOVER team has developed a multi-phased, multi-sectorial implementation strategy of a ceramic water filter factory prototype design.
The study and enhancement of an existing facility in Mashamba will provide a starting point for the development of a replicable design for ceramic water filter factories and landscape interventions in the province of Limpopo and additional rural provinces of South Africa.

Erin Root (M.Arch '11 + MLA '13)in discussion with a community from Limpopo about the water filter factory, summer 2013

Domestic & International Disaster Recovery Housing

The problem of designing for emergency situations in unstable environments is highly complex and requires a great deal of rigor, interdisciplinary collaboration, and entrepreneurship. Initiative reCOVER has designed and fabricated several disaster recovery housing prototypes. As a pedagogical framework, the initiative focuses the students' attention on a finite architectural scope with the intention of ensuring comprehensive and thorough design processes and viable building proposals. Critical variables such as climate and weather, geography, culture and customs, local resources and building techniques, policies and agencies, vulnerability to disasters, and health risks are rigorously analyzed and synthesized. The principal goal for reCOVER is to positively affect and promote the design and building of safe, healthy, and sustainable communities around the world.

UVA team, lead by Sara Harper (BSArch '11) constructing the "Breathe House" (St. Marc, Haiti), summer 2012

Tokyo 2050

Transforming Tokyo into an "Immigration City"
Teppei Iizuka, M.Arch 2013_Thesis
Advisors: Matthew Jull, Peter Waldman

Immigration has become an alternative solution to the problems of a shrinking society. ContemporaryJapanese society is not yet fully open to this option. This experimental project considers how to transform Tokyo into an "immigration city" through a concept of "Mask," which highlights a unique coexistence between immigrants and Japanese people.

What if one proposes an "Immigration Tower" in the heart of Tokyo as a symbol of the times? Would this cause further segregation or provide an opportunity to transform how Japanese people view immigrants? From a historical perspective, Japan used to host immigrants from the West during the Edo period. It did this by providing them a small village where they could reside together and create their own community. This immigrant-based village was called *Dejima*. My project takes this concept a step further, and tries to demonstrate how and with what consequences this type of village could be inserted into the city itself, rather than in peripheral suburbs.

In the year 20XX, Japan actively seeks to become a "country of immigration." This process begins with the establishment of a Ministry of Immigration under a direct provision of the Prime Minister. As the first step, the Ministry develops an "Immigration Tower" in the heart of Tokyo with subsequent support for those newcomers.

Tokyo, Japan
Crisis
Paradigm Shift

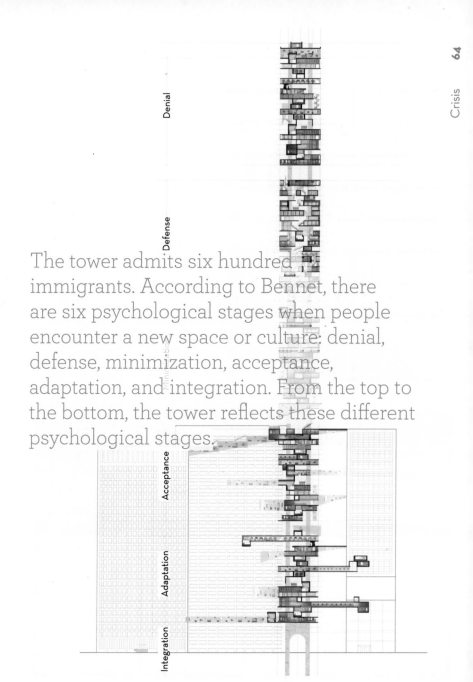

Denial

Defense

The tower admits six hundred
immigrants. According to Bennet, there
are six psychological stages when people
encounter a new space or culture: denial,
defense, minimization, acceptance,
adaptation, and integration. From the top to
the bottom, the tower reflects these different
psychological stages.

Acceptance

Adaptation

Integration

Wind Hill
Future Fit_Dripps_Fall 2012
The intention is to propose a model for a three-dimensional city block by dealing with WIND to increase quality of life in a higher-density city block. Unlike the conventional "pancake," this strategy is meant to elevate/cumulate a rich variety of urban street patterns in Washington, DC. These "paths" for pedestrians as well as wind animate the public ground vertically and make a corresponding relationship between nature and people.

Top: 1. *Rakuchu-Rakugai* (early 17th c.), 2. core of triptych, 3. *Children's Games*, Peter Bruegel (1560), 4. composite
Bottom: 1. Public Space/Masque, 2. Core/Screen, 3. Housing/Mask, 4. composite

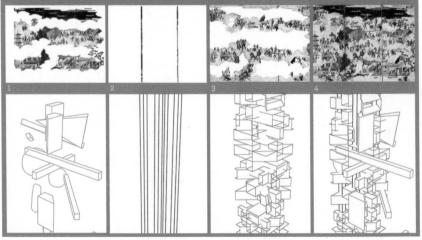

"The return of utopia has not been carried alone by visionary optimism; it has also been shaped by strong dystopian apocalyptic visions that prevailed in the late 1990s. With the turning of the millennium, narratives that had stressed the end gave way to narratives of the after. Indeed, the post-critical, post-tectonic, post-theoretical, post-historical, post-postmodern, and post-industrial have come to mark the landscape of our contemporary architectural debates."

(Contandriopoulos, "Architecture and Utopia in the 21st-Century," 2013)

End of the World

Matthew Jull_Fall 2012_Research Studio

December 21, 2012, marked the end of the Mayan calendar and the completion of a 5125-year cycle. Some believed this date would mark the end of the world, based on predictions that flooding, massive storms, economic collapse, solar flares, earthquakes, super-volcanoes, or Earth's collision with a hidden planet called "Nibiru" would wipe out civilization. An alternative interpretation took this date to mark the start of a new era of physical or spiritual transformation for Earth and its inhabitants. In either case, preparations for this event had been underway for years.

For the last three and a half months leading up to the prophesied day, this studio adopted the lexicon of survivalist culture in a context of increasing uncertainties and shifts both real and imagined—to explore architecture's potential to mediate this impending event. Is this the end of the world, or a new beginning? How can architecture act when confronted with changes whose scale exceeds human control? Ultimately, the studio sought questions more than answers while simultaneously defining a position within the broader cultural and environmental conditions of uncertainty beyond human scale and the architectural possibilities of this increasingly ubiquitous condition.

Charlottesville, Virginia
Crisis
Paradigm Shift

A series of physical concept models exploring spatial responses to uncertainty resulting from forces or events.

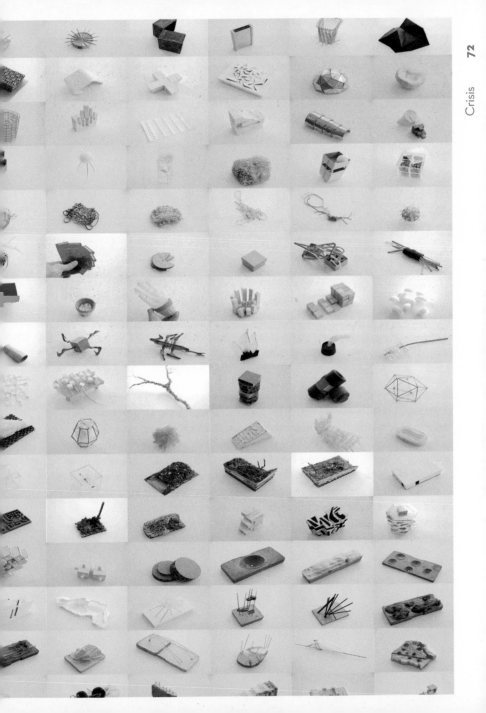

In response to imagined end-of-the world scenarios, a wide range of responses were developed such as opportunism, religious/psychological guidance, protection, autonomous isolated mini-cities, and new centers of government. The last phase involved the design of a single building or complex of buildings for one hundred people who will become either the nucleus of a new beginning or mark a "last stand," containing some aspects of the following program: housing, meditation or religious spaces, broadcast facilities, observation and scientific facilities, cultural and performance spaces, dining areas, and a medical center, in addition to food, water, ventilation, and energy systems.

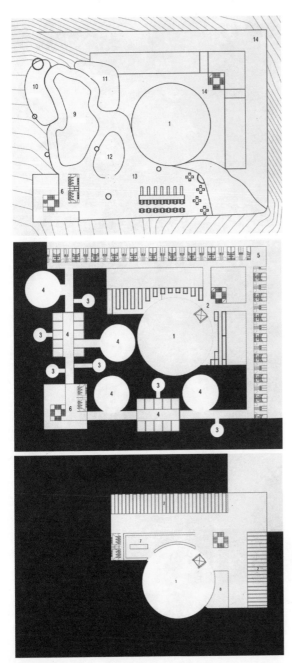

1 Dining
2 Aquaponics
3 Small Baths
4 Large Baths
5 Lounge
6 Changing Rooms
7 Kitchen
8 Storage
9 Pool
10 Hot Bath
11 Warm Bath
12 Cold Bath
13 Library
14 Rooftop Terrace

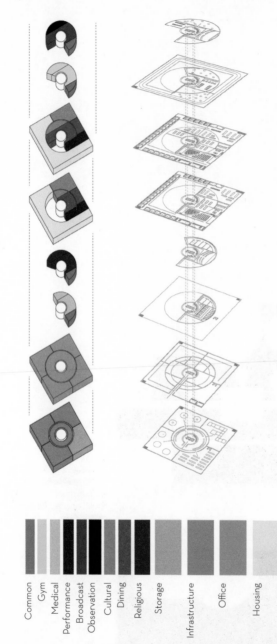

Common
Gym
Medical
Performance
Broadcast
Observation
Cultural
Dining
Religious
Storage

Infrastructure

Office

Housing

Revolver is comprised of individual rotating floor plates housed within a tubular super structure. The floors are able to move through wind power. Each of the floors contains a specific program with portions exposed to the elements.

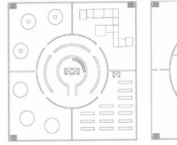  

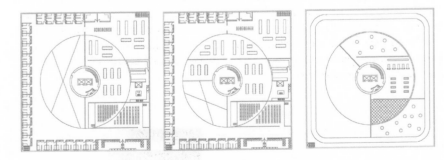

M. Curry

Suburbia

Iñaki Alday and Esther Lorenz_Fall 2012_Research Studio

Suburban growth in the past decades has produced an impossible and unrecogniz-able "popular" style which entails the erasure of landscapes and the application of standard solutions, which are rather related to a funny combination of Disney and *The Simpsons* than to any urban, landscape, or architectural thought. Urged by eco-nomic and ecological crisis, this studio ventures a design research into alternative concepts of suburbia. The typical growth of new suburbia in North America produc-es pseudo-communities with little variations across different latitudes. The territory is deprived of its qualities and distinctive traces in order to be easily transformed into a sort of chessboard. In response, this studio researches the design of urban forms in which public space and landscape become the driving forces to develop a distinctive identity and urban quality. We want to approach buildable land as a "place," not generic sites ready for the work of heavy bulldozers. The existing fields, microtopographies, water systems, agricultural production, and forests provide con-ditions and constraints, thus opportunities and new demands. New opportunities linked to infrastructural and transportation operations are arising in several places. The construction of new light trains allows us to imagine a new city of distributed and well-connected hubs of a higher density and with their own identity, as opposed to the usual central skyline of towers surrounded by thousands or millions of acres of undifferentiated urban sprawl. The goal of proposing a new way of developing a city is related to an understanding of the existing landscape and the impact of the creation of a new layer of landscape, to the survey of existing forms of mobility and metropolitan links, and to the analysis of densities and the mixture of uses. At a larger scale, the research seeks to find a responsible answer in terms of territory and overall planning strategy. At a smaller, human scale, the quality of life, both inside the home and outside in the urban space and the landscape, are of major concern. The problem is understood in its overall complexity as well as in relation to the individual urban experience.

Northern Virginia
Crisis
Paradigm Shift/System

N. Cronauer, B. Porada

The first edition of the "Suburbia Studio" (spring 2012, instructors Iñaki Alday / Tat Bonvehi) took place in Forney, located in the Sunbelt state of Texas, which is currently the fastest growing state in the United States. The studio proposed six models for a new city, responding to infrastructures and transportation, to landscape and productive ground, to water and topography, to health and culture, to complexity and mixed uses, or to density and urban condition.

Suburbia Studio 2, fall 2012

This second edition of the "Suburbia Studio" continues the design research in a new geographic, demographic, economic, and infrastructural context: Northern Virginia. The Dulles Metrorail Corridor project formed the background for the studio investigation. A new metro line—the "Silver Line"—is planned to branch off the existing Orange Line to form a direct connection between the center of Washington, DC, and the airport, and beyond. Phase 1 is currently under construction. The studio looks at the line as a whole but with a particular focus on phase 2, still in the planning stage. Each of the locations for the six new stations in phase 2 has its own characteristics in terms of topography, program, density, and administrative affiliation. The current station plans understand the station as a simple interchange infrastructure between the private car and the metro, thus increasing the barrier that the highway and the rail tracks are creating in the territory without adding any kind of additional value and ignoring the specifics of the landscape, geography, and the existing settlement pattern. The fact that the highway has formed an environmental nuisance and a hard and impermeable edge during decades of suburban development, pushing its sites into a condition of periphery, might have contributed to the skepticism towards the usefulness and economic viability of the metro rail project. The suburbia studio aims to take a more provocative and proactive stand. It starts from the assumption that each of these new stations offers more potential than just the provision of a simple intermodal interface. On the contrary, the new train line and its stations could become the incubators for a new interpretation of suburban life; they offer the opportunity to create new "subcities" with a distinct character. The studio explores this potential on the scale of the whole line, on a district scale around the new stations, and on the scale of the station itself. Students are asked to develop a strong argument for their vision of "retrofitting suburbia" (Dunham-Jones and Williamson, 2009), establishing a conceptual thread throughout these scales which would render the new infrastructure meaningful in regard to the future development of the affected suburban communities. The projects deal with selected issues of contemporary American suburbs such as environmental sustainability, mobility, changing social structures, work-life pattern, affordability, communication, etc., as well as with opportunities arising from the specific sites, such as connectivity, the interplay of various modes of movement, programmatic and spatial intensification, the creation of new public spaces, and a sensitive approach to landscape.

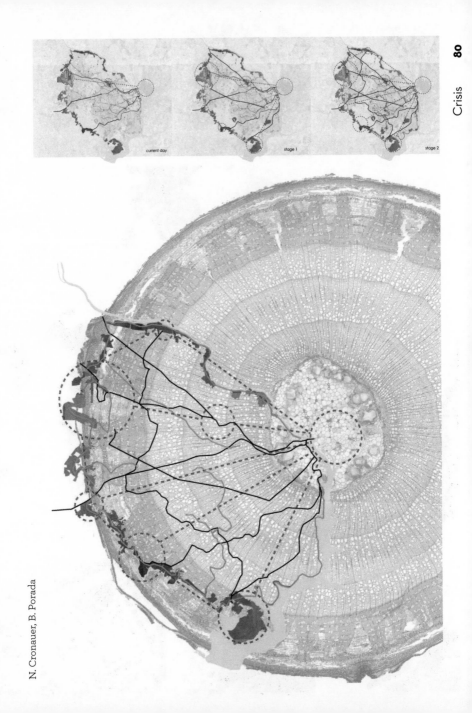

N. Cronauer, B. Porada

current day

stage 1

stage 2

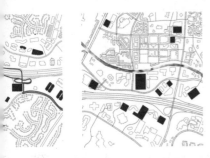

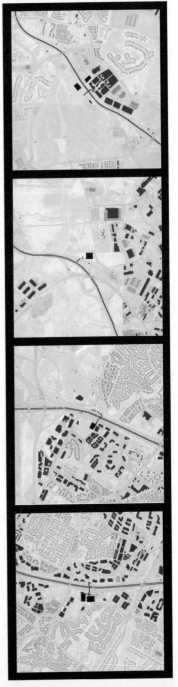

By creating a Civic Corridor for Development, the scheme strengthens an existing commercial space to connect to the new metro stop for Reston by promoting a system of lots and applicable programs.

N. Connors, A. Walker

"The other factor is the rapid advancement of organizations in modern civilized society brought about by the modern communication system, informationa technology, and the sharp reflection of this phenomenon on spatial organization. In modern civilized society, space is a communication field, and it is becoming more and more organic with the development of the communication system. . . .Creating an architecture and a city may be called a process of making the communication network visible in a space... We can say that the spatial organization is a network of energy and communication."

(Kenzo Tange [1966], qtd. in Wigley, "Network Fever," 2001)

"In the past years, we have forgotten that architecture is also about the hope of a different and better future, and this is its real political and social function.

This hope cannot be found in traditional formulas; the issue is no longer to design ideal cities or plans. The first lesson of history is to try not to repeat itself; a new kind of utopian perspective is needed today. Its starting point must be present-day conditions, one of which is the blurring between nature and technology.

Reinventing utopia might ultimately not only be about sustainability or contemporary emergencies ... these issues are of course absolutely imperative, but we need also improve the linking of digital imagery to reality. What radically different future lies in such links ? This may prove to be one of the questions architecture has to address today."

(Picon, "Learning From Utopia, Contemporary Architecture and the Quest for Political and Social Relevance," 2013)

Future Fit

Robin Dripps_Fall 2012_Research Studio

Future Fit describes how existing urban conditions can be augmented and radically changed by strategies of addition, incision, weaving, and careful subtraction to create thick gradient spatial networks overlaid on and engaging existing construction that harvest and distribute resources while supporting new open and responsive patterns of movement and connectivity. Based on the premise that current urban form and attendant processes are incapable of sustaining themselves ecologically and socially, the work of this studio engages in rigorous research and design, using a wide range of tools including advanced modes of computation in order to propose and test interventions at multiple scales and time frames. The resulting work is expected to be exemplary as a model for rethinking urban form and process and how these engage nature.

Much focus is directed towards rethinking the idea and actuality of infrastructure. Is it possible to conceive of infrastructure as embedded and integral to all aspects and scales of architecture, landscape architecture, and urban structure? What is the possibility for a hybrid infrastructure of constructed and natural processes? Can infrastructure be emergent, responsive, self-regulating, and inherently self-sustaining? If infrastructure becomes spatial, can this be an effective and poetic foundation for a new architecture? The work is highly speculative in the manner of the provocations of Archigram, Superstudio, and the Metabolists, but differs, however, in terms of the background research, the use of advanced technologies and material practices, and a better appreciation and understanding of natural process so that the results can be both provocative and pragmatic.

Washington, DC
Crisis
Paradigm Shift / System

Can infrastructure be emergent, responsive, self-regulating, and inherently self-sustaining?

The scale of research and design proposals spans a range from complex, urban-scale networks to infrastructural architecture/landscapes, including surfaces, mechanisms, and other artifacts capable of responding to local environmental and social flux, harvesting, storing, and distributing resources, and facilitating alternate modes of connectivity and social aggregation. This multiyear research studio begins in Washington, DC (taking the capital city as a world stage on which to demonstrate substantial new directions), with inventive mapping, modeling, and speculative analysis through iterative design proposals. Students initiate and develop their particular area of research, define the methods, and speculate on modes of representation.

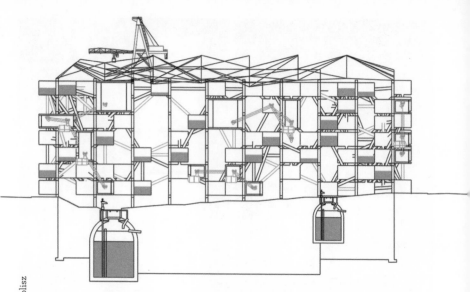

P. Golisz

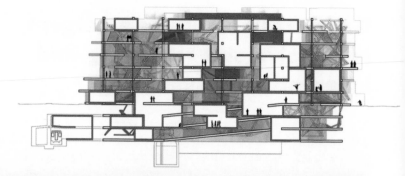

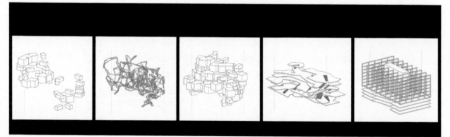

Urban InfrastructuralThreshold/Future Fit

Qiufan Wu, M.Arch 2013
Advisors: Robin Dripps, Charlie Menefee, Bill Sherman

The project describes an emergent model of an urban public space system based on rethinking the relationship between urban public life and infrastructure. It catalyzes local connectivity and animates self-sustaining urban life, which establishes the condition for a sustainable urban metabolism. Central to sustaining ourselves both ecologically and socially, the concept of a threshold not only defines the spatial zone negotiating between public and private, street and building; it also helps us to address future challenges such as the depletion of water and energy resources, population pressure, social fragmentation, or even climate change.

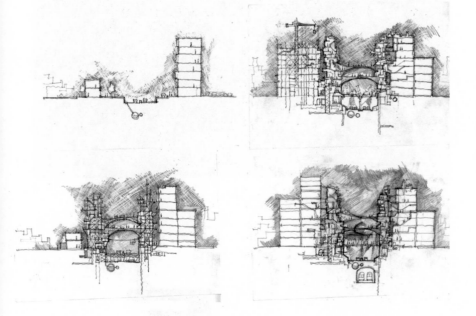

Parametric Fiction

Lucia Phinney_Spring 2013_Research Studio

The dystopian and semi-abandoned cities of twenty-first-century America, with their dependence on vulnerable supply networks and an increasing susceptibility to weather-related calamities, here form the territory for a retelling of Homer's *Odyssey*. Many careful speculative rereadings of this text lead to urban landscapes and other constructs for Odysseus's American homecoming. Textual themes, structures, and descriptions form the basis for a sequence of projects addressing the relationship of verbal to spatial narrative, waste, dystopia, resilience, evolody and conservation, chronos and hora, atmospheric phenomena, and human conceptions of nature.

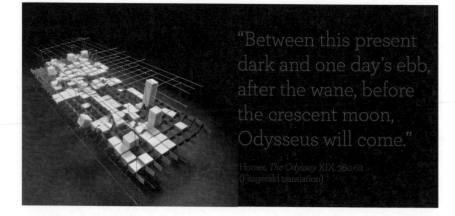

"Between this present dark and one day's ebb, after the wane, before the crescent moon, Odysseus will come."

Homer, *The Odyssey* XIX. 360-62 (Fitzgerald translation)

Baltimore, Maryland
Crisis
Paradigm Shift

E. Ashby

QuasiObjects/ WorldObjects/ HyperObjects

New Classification of the Urban Metabolism
Woltz Symposium

The past decade has seen widespread development of forms of urban analysis and design based on various material, environmental, economic, and social flows. While this approach has supplanted our discussion of the city as fixed, our classification system has lagged behind in its transformation. In suggesting the term *urban metabolism*, we seek new classifications of environmental flows to assist us to think, to harvest, and to relate. In these environmental flows, soil and earth, green and energy, building services and architecture are not divided; they form complex entities.

This symposium asks participants to gather thoughts on a range of entities under the general notion of "objects"—temporarily distanced from moral and aesthetic judgments pronounced on them and modifications made to them in response to these judgments—to reconstitute a place of humanity in them. As both creators and the recipients of these hugely complex systems, human beings face the problem of how to classify themselves beyond humanism; in seeking equality in representations in the parliament of things, we must first revise our categories of knowledge to embrace what may be described as a nature/culture/infrastructure amalgam. In order to frame the discussion, we are using three "objects" to delineate a different landscape within which this symposium takes place.

INVITED PANELISTS

Susanne Hauser PhD
Berlin University of the Arts, Germany

Claire Pentecost
The School of the Art Institute of Chicago

Niels Albertsen PhD
University Aarhus Denmark

Ryan Bishop PhD
University of Southampton

Seth Denizen
University of Hong Kong

Martin Felsen
UrbanLab, Chicago

Scott Lash PhD
Goldsmiths, University of London

Dirk Sijmons PhD
TU Delft - H+N+S Amsterdam, Netherlands

RESPONDENTS University of Virginia

Sheila Crane PhD
Assistant Professor in Architectural History

Robin Dripps
Professor in Architecture

Teresa Gali
Associate Professor in Landscape Architecture

Beth Meyer
Associate Professor in Landscape Architecture

Matthew Jull PhD
Assistant Professor in Architecture

Bill Sherman
Associate Professor in Architecture

ORGANIZING COMMITTEE

Jorg Sieweke, Organizer
Assistant Professor in Landscape Architecture

Nana Last PhD, Committee
Associate Professor in Architecture

Shiqiao Li PhD, Committee
Professor in Architecture

Two Ways to Organize, 2006 (Detail), Leslie Shows

PHANTOM. *Mies as Rendered Society*. Andrés Jaque / Office for Political Innovation, Barcelona Pavilion

CF000478, from the series *Midway: Message from the Gyre*, Chris Jordan

QuasiObjects

What complex entities and hybrid networks have either recently emerged or have existed but were neglected or denied under modernity? How can we pivot environmental artifacts such as the manicured lawn and the conditioned air between the human and the nonhuman, between subject and object? By making central the processes of configurations of each other, can we begin to reimagine our understanding of human/nature by bringing to the fore the marginalized and the neglected?

WorldObjects

If we focus on a new set of previously marginalized entities, what status are they to be given? Can we, for example, expand our concept of legal subjects to nonhumans, as if in a historical progression of acknowledging other legal subjects from white males to women, children, and people of color? What are the potential nonhuman legal subjects we might acknowledge in this new framework? Fish in the world's oceans? Seedbanks? Fertile soils or farmland?

HyperObjects

How do we situate or theorize a set of material entities that, while made by us, elude or defy established human temporal and spatial scales? What new modes of operating or realms of practice do such things as nuclear waste surfacing in Louisiana salt-domes, sinkholes, the ever-growing plastic trash vortex in the Pacific Ocean, or Greenland's melting icecaps bear upon our understanding of and approaches to the urban metabolism?

My Hair Is at MoMA PS1 2013

TempAgency_Spring 2013_Finalists, MoMA PS1 Young Architects Program

"My Hair Is at MoMA PS1" is a project about the waste everyone produces: our hair. It is an element that links us, divides us, fascinates us, and reflects our individual and cultural diversity. This project aims at diverting hair as a material waste stream and utilizing the cultural and architectural potential of our hair's thermal, acoustic, and structural qualities. Working in collaboration with material scientists, hair stylists, medical doctors, and engineers, we revive and transform waste hair into a dynamic, interactive, and resilient modular canvas. This is a project about curating this process and manufacturing the power and spatial typologies of this living material.

The process we propose has four phases: hair collection, treatment, assembly, and installation. TempAgency partnered with over 120 New York City hair salons and barbershops and collected a total amount of eighty cubic feet of hair for a period of five days. Collected hair was carefully inspected, sanitized, dyed, and bound with customized weather-proof, fire-retardant silicone, affixed to light and rigid metal mesh, then finally to fiberglass poles. Horizontal and vertical variations of the hair rollers offer six distinct stage-like environments in the MoMA PS1 courtyards—"Cut," "Tease," "Brush," "Part," "Wash," and "Love Cave"— and provide shade, seating, and water as well as intense yet flexible spaces for Expo1, Warm-Up, and barbershop for the ultimate cooldown. With a color-coded tagging system, each hair roller is also a representation of an individual salon or barbershop from one of five boroughs, which together act as a map of the hair taxonomy of the city. The tags guide visitors on a quest to find their own hair and salons/barbershops in the MoMA PS1 courtyards. This is a landscape of serendipity, overlaid with scientific and tactile explorations of material and information, and ultimately an architectural expression of renewed life.

New York City, New York
Crisis
System

There are over four thousand hair salons and barbershops in the five boroughs of New York City. Each salon produces up to four cubic feet of hair clippings daily, and nearly all of it ends up in a landfill; this material that once signified diversity, character, and collective identity is readily forgotten and discarded.

TempAgency is a design/research collaborative between Kutonotuk (Leena Cho and Matthew Jull) and mcdowellespinosa (Rychiee Espinosa and Seth McDowell). TempAgency's work lies at the intersection of architecture, landscape architecture, urbanism, product design, and an array of interrelated forces that shape the built environment from the scale of the object and the body to that of the city and the continent. Combining expertise linking materials, politics, and science, the collaboration defines a unique and critical vision for the future of sustainability.
Student team: Jake Fox, Aaron Gahr, Ben Gregory, Teppei Iizuka, Gwen McGinn, Matthew Pinyan

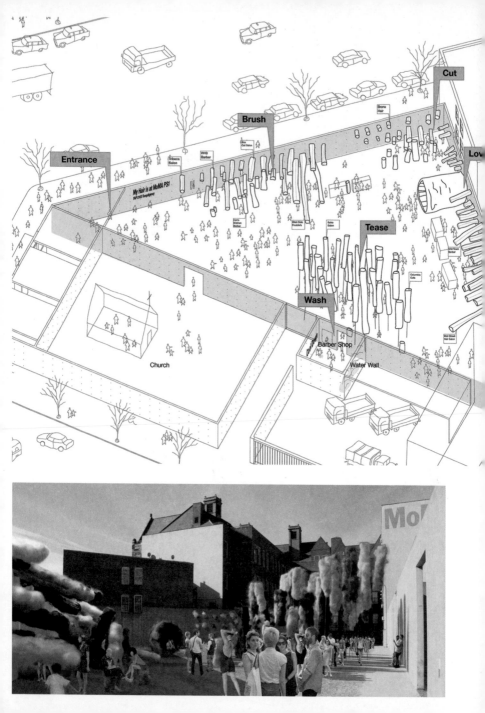

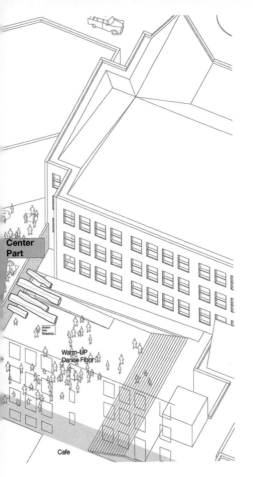

Center
Part

Warm-UP
Dance Floor

Cafe

Trash Tectonics

Upcycled Environments for Architecture and Art
Seth McDowell_Spring 2013_Research Studio

TRASH TECTONICS is a design research studio that focuses on the transformation of waste, excess, and the ordinary into new spatial and material realities.

In this studio, students work predominantly at full scale to investigate new material prototypes and assemblies developed from collected waste products. Material transformation and customization are employed as a methodology for extending material life, as discarded and outgrown waste becomes precise construction material.

The work of the studio is prompted by four questions. What if architecture was constructed from 99 percent upcycled materials? What if spatial formation emerged directly from material and assembly logics? What if we eliminate the need for raw material and banish all waste? What if design was to occur simultaneously with building?

Upcycling is the process of converting waste materials and products into new materials of better quality and environmental value. TRASH TECTONICS is a design studio structured as a construction laboratory investigating the opportunities for upcycling waste and postconsumer products for spatial and architectural purposes. The ecological mandate of the work is to develop

[siteless]
Crisis
System

K. Badlato + E. Burch + E. Scott

methods and processes for remediation by transforming waste into building material. Emphasis is placed on developing energy-efficient methods for material transformation rather than relying on energy intensive procedures that reprocess tahe material compositions. Thus a ready-made approach is prioritized and transformation is achieved by low-tech and innovative strategies of assembly. Upcycling is about the way we remake things. TRASH TECHTONICS takes the format of a construction laboratory rather than a design studio. Design occurs simultaneously with the act of building and making. The process privileges the tangible over the intangible; the built over the drawing. This laboratory operates outside of the abstraction of scale and continuously explores the consequences of design and construction at a one-to-one scale. Construction is an exercise of both mind and body. The semester is organized as a series of Free Builds. *Free Build* has two meanings: to build with little or no monetary expenses for material or labor and to build without a master plan or predetermined form. Form and organization emerges from local conditions and decisions.

N. Cronauer + A. Picciano

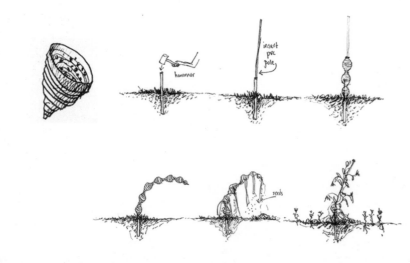

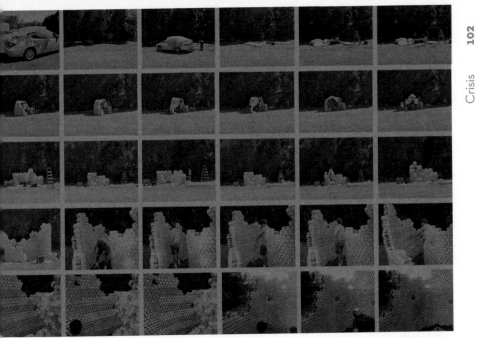

K. Badlato + E. Burch + E. Scott

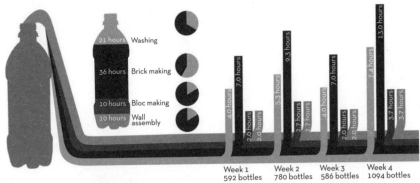

21 hours — Washing

36 hours — Brick making

10 hours — Bloc making

10 hours — Wall assembly

Week 1
592 bottles — 4.0 hours, 7.0 hours

Week 2
780 bottles — 5.3 hours, 2.7 hours, 2.7 hours, 9.3 hours

Week 3
586 bottles — 4.0 hours, 2.0 hours, 2.0 hours, 7.0 hours

Week 4
1094 bottles — 13.0 hours, 7.4 hours, 3.7 hours, 3.7 hours

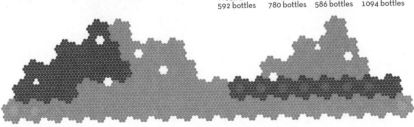

"Whereas the constant feedback loops of actualization and visualization render nature as an assembly of information processing, architects reinforce the belief in harnessing such mechanisms using powerful computational means while at the same time considering the potentially repressive conditions associated with technology. This dual nature of information engenders a perception of reality that we propose to call 'atopia' in reference to a reality deprived of limits between nature and culture, ecosystems and technological networks, organic and robotic process. Pressured by the 'informatization' of the architectural project, the atopian model suggests that nature can no longer be defined in terms of a duality between natural and artificial but is rather incorporated into a virtual assembly of operations."

(Sprecher & Leblanc, "Dissipative Architecture, The Informed Nature of Atopia," 2013)

Soft Surface Operations

Lucia Phinney_Fall 2012_Seminar
Molly Baum, M.Arch 2013 + Lain Lai Jiang, M.Arch 2014

The barnacle field is an array of objects deployed across a terrain.
Activated by chemical and proximity sensors, they detect aerial and aqueous
pollutants. Surfaces emerging from individual barnacles in response to these
stimuli detect environmental conditions and mitigate polluting effects.
The physical response is accomplished with Miga Motor shape memory alloy
technology. The thin, powerful, and lightweight Miga creates a linear motion
that is magnified through linkages. The barnacle field is a prototype for
potential applications ranging from multilevel building neighborhoods
to teacup fleets to be activated during flood events.

Stasis

Cities are built according to principles of stability but make manifest the dynamic processes through which the public realm and the private domain interact and overlap.

The rigor of the public institution and the utility and ubiquity of spaces of habitation remain constant as stabilizers in the face of change and provide the framework for experiments in materiality, tectonics, spatial structures, programmatic hybridities...

What role do current technologies play in animating part-to-whole relationships to operate as dynamic scalable and expandable systems that have the capacity to respond to complex programmatic and site conditions? (Stasis 129)

To what extent can information technology impact the cultural forces that shape material production? (Stasis 141)

How do the city and the public institution inform and transform each other? (Stasis 177)

How can existing social trends become catalysts for urban revitalization, social mobility and improved ecological performance? (Stasis 181)

Classicism Is Not What You Think It Is

Cammy Brothers_Department of Architectural History

Classical architecture, conventionally understood, is defined by norms, rules, and canonical models. Any visitor to Washington, DC, knows that it is the language of authority and power. But what if that Greco-Roman architectural tradition were less rule-bound and regular than generally imagined?

This possibility emerges from any close examination of ancient architecture and points to an important insight: the view of classical architecture that has been passed on through the centuries is extremely selective and has favored the normative over the exceptional.

While the formation of the classical tradition is a long and complex story, an important early point in this narrative occurred in the Renaissance. In the era before schools of architecture were established, architects sought their education among the ruins of Rome. Knowledge of Roman monuments was highly prized among patrons, and architects able to demonstrate this through their books of drawings put themselves at a considerable professional advantage. According to some accounts, the publication in 1486 by Giovanni Sulpizio da Veroli of the first authoritative version of the ancient author Vitruvius was a watershed moment. Prior to its publication, the text—the only surviving verbal account of Roman architecture—had been known only through a series of corrupted manuscripts. After its publication, many architects sought to understand the text by attempting to find corollaries to the forms and principles Vitruvius described among the monuments and fragments of ancient Rome. While aspects of this account are probably correct, the ruins and monuments themselves also exerted an irresistible pull on architects.

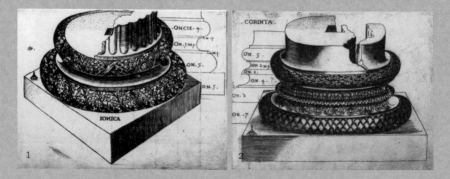

The intense lure of Roman monuments for Renaissance architects helps explain the discrepancy between the types of buildings and details they drew and those described by Vitruvius. In many ways, the physical remains of ancient Rome pointed in different directions than the text of Vitruvius, and the tensions between these directions constituted a significant theme of our show. Vitruvius, writing in the first century BCE at the dawn of the imperial age of Augustus, looked back admiringly to the republican era of architecture, little of which survived into the sixteenth century. As a result, there was not much correspondence between what the text described and what Renaissance architects could see around Rome. Some architects, such as Serlio, commented directly on this, but in most cases the disjunction was unresolved and unstated.

An exhibition mounted at the University of Virginia Museum of Art in collaboration with Michael Waters in August 2011, "Variety, Archaeology and Ornament: Architectural Prints from Column to Cornice," attempted to complicate the history of classical architecture.[1] The prints that form the core of the show, a set of twenty-three architectural prints by the person known as "Master G.A. with the Caltrop," indicate that a lively interest in noncanonical, non-Vitruvian details survived well into the sixteenth century. Other similar sets of prints representing architectural details, such as those by the Master P.S. or by Antonio Salamanca, were produced around the same time and reflect similar concerns. The propagation, in print form, of anomalous, highly ornamented architectural details does more than contradict the idea that all architects were striving to understand and emulate Vitruvius. At the most fundamental level, it challenges the notion that the classical language of architecture is based on a limited set of models. We have come to understand the five orders—Doric, Ionic, Corinthian, Composite, and Tuscan—as an inclusive list.

1. The exhibition was accompanied by a catalogue, published digitally on the Museum website, from which this text is derived. Michael Waters a recipient of a Masters in Architectural History from the University of Virginia and a Ph.D. candidate at New York University.

.CORINTIA.

1. All engravings are from the University of Virginia Art Museum.
2. Ionic base, c. 1537
   Engraving, 5 1/4 x 7 3/16 in
   Corinthian base from the
3. Lateran Baptistery, Rome, c. 1537,
   Engraving, 5 1/8 x 6 7/8 in
   Corinthian base, c. 1537
   Engraving, 5 1/8 x 6 3/4 in

While the nature of ornament, the aesthetics of variety, and the meaning of the canon are of general interest to historians and architects, they also have particular resonance at the University of Virginia. The centrality of Jefferson's Lawn to the life and collective imagination of the University makes the classical tradition both keenly felt and highly contested.

The Master G.A. prints indicate that a much wider range of models for the orders was known throughout the sixteenth century, and that the changes wrought by the transition from drawing to print were not as drastic as are often thought. They suggest that the print medium did not intrinsically veer towards canonical forms, but rather that print could be used to propagate a tradition favoring ornamental designs that otherwise existed only in scattered books of drawings. The story these prints tell is a surprising one: they suggest that rather than the commonplace idea that all Renaissance architecture was moving in the direction of the formation of a canon of ancient monuments, a standard mode of representation, and the authoritative definition of the classical orders as described by Vitruvius, a strong and vibrant alternative existed as well. They illustrate an interest in highly ornamental and unusual ancient details that goes against the Vitruvian ideas that Palladio would eventually embrace. While the nature of ornament, the aesthetics of variety, and the meaning of the canon are of general interest to historians and architects, they also have particular resonance at the University of Virginia. The centrality of Jefferson's Lawn to the life and collective imagination of the University makes the classical tradition both keenly felt and highly contested. Despite having based his interpretation of the classical tradition on books rather than on a direct encounter with Rome, Jefferson embraced the broadest interpretation of its legacy, emphatically displaying a range of capitals and columns in each of the Lawn's pavilions. In this regard at least, the inclusive understanding of the canon and the celebration of variety demonstrated by the artists, architects, and printmakers in our show are in keeping with the aesthetic values on display in the Lawn. It is our hope that on this site in particular, the exhibition would fuel the ongoing discussion and debate surrounding the legacy, interpretation, and uses of classicism.

All engravings are from
the University of Virginia
Art Museum.
4. Basket capital with fruit and
   satyr head, c. 1537
5. Capital with peapod volutes
   and satyr head, c. 1537
   Engraving, 5 3/16 x 6 1/8 in
6. Capital with ram's heads and
   masks, c. 1537
   Engraving, 6 3/4 x 6 in

The Architectural Detail

Princeton Architectural Press, 2011

Edward Ford_Department of Architecture

While there are a large number of publications on architectural details and
a variety of professional manuals on the subject, there is no significant body
on theory of the detail. In fact, there is a widespread belief that such a theory
is both irrelevant and unnecessary. Le Corbusier and Paul Rudolph said that
there are no details. Others see such an exploration as dangerous. Zaha Hadid
and Greg Lynn have declared the detail a fetish. To Rem Koolhaas details
are ornament and must be dispensed with. *The Architectural Detail* seeks
to demonstrate that details are not merely technically but architecturally
necessary. The book is both definitive in exploring the existing approaches
and prescriptive in arguing for detailing as a process that can be at times
independent of the design of the larger work. The five sections of the book
analyze and evaluate five definitions of detail: the non-detail, the motific
detail, the detail as structural representation, the detail as joint, and the
autonomous detail. The drawing illustrations employ a hybrid technology,
combining original hand-drawn, ink-on-paper drawings with a series of
digital photographs taken from the same angles. The result is a series of
precise representations of the featured buildings. The brick shown on the
drawings is not a "fill" option in AutoCAD; the reflections in the glass are not
computer generated. Both are drawn from the actual buildings.
While a typical modernist attitude acknowledges the technical necessity
of detailing, the articulated detail, the visible manifestation of a solution
to a technical problem—the door frame or the exposed fastener—must be
avoided. Detailing is the elimination of the visible minutiae of construction
in the service of simplicity of form. The abstraction of the whole requires the
abstraction of the part.

Detailing at its best is a mediation between the
way in which we see a building and the way we feel
a building, between abstraction and animation,
between material reality and idealized form.

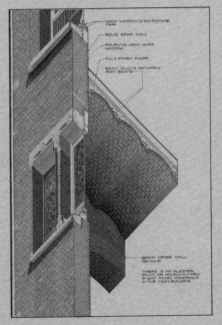

WOOD WINDOW W/ SANDSTONE TRIM
SOLID BRICK WALL
RELIEVING ARCH OVER WINDOW
FILL & FINISH FLOOR
BRICK VAULTS BETWEEN IRON BEAMS

BRICK CROSS WALL BEYOND

THERE IS NO PLASTER, PAINT OR PANELING + FEW IF ANY FINISH MATERIALS IN THE MAIN BUILDING

Fig. 1 Wall Section
Amsterdam Stock Exchange, H.P. Berlage,
Amsterdam, Netherlands, 1903

An opposing theory argues that visible details are essential. This might be called the DNA theory, in which the detail is the part from which the whole is generated. This takes the form of the repetitive motif—sometimes technical, sometimes decorative—as in the work of Frank Lloyd Wright. Fay Jones's Thorncrown Chapel is thus generated from the diamond-shaped joint of the trusses. A third theory of the detail, associated with Mies van der Rohe, sees the detail as a structural symbol, a necessary device when one wishes to express structure but is required for technical reasons to conceal it. This is illustrated by the work of Bernard Maybeck, sometimes explicitly through exposed construction, sometimes symbolically through the design of its cladding.

All of these theories assume detailing is the act of carrying the ideas of the larger building into its small-scale elements. It is simply a question of consistency. All are flawed. The absolute rejection of detail is naïve in its erroneous faith in the simplicity of modern construction. Consistency leads inevitably to styling and denial of scale. The motif easily becomes decoration, and the structural symbol all too easily becomes the structural deception. But problems aside, we must begin by understanding that details are the mechanism for basic architectural understandings and find alternative definitions that get at the heart of this second level of architecture.

The first of these alternatives is the idea, advocated by Louis Kahn, that the detail is the joint. This is not an issue of technology but of aesthetics. While any building has a certain number of real parts, it has a much smaller number of perceptible parts and the articulated detail is that which establishes the perception of those parts. A joint by Craig Elwood and one by Eduardo Souto de Moura illustrate this difference. One unites the parts; one divides them. In the thinking of historians like Heinrich Wolfflin and Erwin Panofsky and of architects such as Kahn and Enric Miralles, the relationship of the architectural part to the architectural whole has been construed as a metaphor for a larger order—an order of society, of spirituality, of thought, of political repression or democratic ideology—and the joint is the way in which these meanings are established. Thus the question is not whether joints can be eliminated or disguised but how architectural meaning is to be established without them. But understanding the joint in this way is only part of the solution. The articulated joint is part of a larger class of dissonant details that speak of fragmentation and incompleteness in a building that expresses solidity and permanence. The dissonant detail is autonomous; it mediates between the contradictory ways we understand a building—as an abstraction and a material reality, as an assembly and as a monolith, as parts and as a whole. Autonomous details may be joints, structural elements, or any other constructional necessity, but in any form they signify animation, impermanence, and materiality within buildings that speak of stasis, stability, and abstraction. They are by definition inconsistent. This is the second alternative definition: the detail that introduces themes counter to those of the building. The sculptural eruptions that are the handrails and door handles of Asplund and the rustic columns of Aalto exemplify this alternative level of design, that of the detail that is autonomous, following its own rules, establishing its own histories and independent of the larger building. Detailing at its best mediates between the way in which we see a building and the way we feel a building, between abstraction and animation, between idealized form and material reality. At its best the detail emerges from the purposeful production of an inconsistent, imperfect, or exceptional part, and while this is often done with an eye toward reconciling the conflicting perceptual demands we make of buildings, it is more likely to make these differences apparent. Detailing that is stylized, perfect, or motific will succeed only where it is inconsistent, imperfect, or exaggerated. The good detail is not consistent, but nonconforming; not typical, but exceptional; not doctrinaire, but heretical; not the continuation of an idea, but its termination, and the beginning of another.

The five sections of the book analyze and evaluate five definitions of detail: the non-detail, the motific detail, the detail as structural representation, the detail as joint, and the autonomous detail.

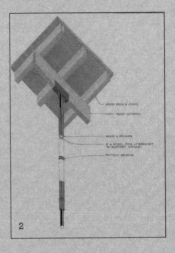

2

Fig. 2 Column First Unitarian Church, A.C. Schweinfurth, Berkeley, California, 1898.
Fig. 3 Construction Sequences of Precast Columns Unity Temple, Frank Lloyd Wright, Oak Park, Illinois, 1908.
Fig. 4 Wall Sections
Top: Rosen House, Craig Ellwood, Brentwood, California, 1963.
Bottom: Residential Block on the Rua do Teatro, Souto de Moura, Porto, Portugal, 1995.

"Ford employed a hybrid technology to produce the drawings included in this exhibit, combining meticulously hand-drawn, original ink-on-paper drawings of buildings with a series of digital photographs he had taken at exactly the same angles. The result is a series of exactly accurate representations of the featured buildings; the shadows are not estimated, they are exactly as pictured in Ford's photographs. The brick shown on the drawings is not a 'fill' option in Auto-CAD; it is exactly as pictured in Ford's photographs."
Jane Ford, *UVA Today*, Feb 15, 2011.

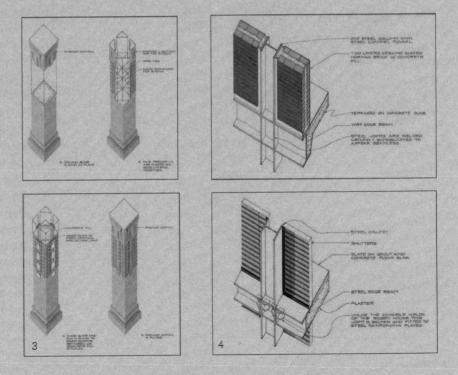

3

4

"What precisely is an architectural detail?
… What is the correct relationship of the
architectural part to the architectural whole?
Is consistency of part and whole desirable
aesthetically or economically?"

(Ford, *The Architectural Detail*, 2011)

"Details are much more than subordinate elements: they can be regarded as the minimal units of signification in the architectural production of meanings. These units have been singled out in spatial cells or in elements of composition, in modules or in measures, in the alternating of void and solid, or in the relationship between inside and outside."

(Frascari, "The Tell-the-Tale Detail," 1996)

Connections on Uncertain Ground

The Cape Cod Studio

Edward Ford_Fall 2012_Research Studio

An exercise in the generation of form not from context, not from site, not from program or fashion or history or precedent, but from the nature of materials and the processes by which they are assembled—from joints.

OBJECTIVES We all design the same way. We begin with the large and go to the small. We begin with the ecosystem and work our way down to the detail. We decide on the form and then we select the material. We solve all the big problems and then we figure out how to put in columns and beams and what to make them out of and how to join them together. Could you design a building in the opposite direction? Could you begin with the small and go to the large? Could you begin with a material and determine the form? Could you begin with a joint and grow a building out of that joint? This studio aims to do the latter: to study a joint, to study the material through the joint, and to determine the building out of both.

The first exercise is to generate forms from joints drawn from vernacular architecture and architectural history. The structures are similar to buildings but have no functional purpose. The second step is to generate larger-scale structures from these joints. These structures have minimal functional requirements other than shelter.

The lessons of the first two exercises are then applied to the design of new facilities at the Cape Cod National Seashore. Many of the existing beach service

Cape Cod, Massachusetts
Stasis
Generative Detail / System

buildings at Cape Cod National Seashore must be replaced because shifting dunes have undermined their foundations, but if replaced by permanent buildings they will soon be below flood levels.

The Herring Cove Complex near Provincetown, Massachusetts was constructed in the 1950s as a state park headquarters. The sand in front of the structures is being washed away by the tides of Cape Cod Bay. Foundations are settling and cracking, making the buildings unstable and unsafe.

The Nauset Light Beach Bath Houses in Easton, Massachusetts are dramatically situated on cliffs forty feet above the sea, but the land is unstable. The original structures built in 1960 have already been rebuilt once due to erosion (in 1986) and if present trends continue—over three feet of horizontal shoreline erosion per year—the beach house complex will fall into the ocean in the next three to ten years.

The project is to remove these structures and replace them with a new building system that can be relocated in the future as the shore continues to erode. Programs will be similar: bathrooms, dressing rooms, lifeguard station, first-aid room, snack bar, and boat house, as well as office and storage space.

STRATEGIES These examples and similar conditions at other National Parks suggest that over the coming years the Park Service will be best served by a nonstandard approach to the placing of buildings on the land, an architecture that is smaller in scale, more flexible in its use, and movable in location. Such architecture would make less of a mark on the land, consume little or no energy, produce little or no waste, and could be removed or relocated with changing conditions. It would have foundation systems that are minimal and adaptable, use construction systems that allowed for a minimum of heavy equipment, be constructed of sustainable materials, and use energy systems suitable for remote locations. It could be closed, moved, or compacted in the off-season and in inclement weather. It might be prefabricated; it might be modular. It might be lightweight and retractable; it might be collapsible and portable. This studio explores facilities that will be less permanent and more flexible, structures that would in all locations make the smallest intervention, and that might, in time, disappear altogether. The intent is not to design a universal, standardized, context-indifferent prototype. The proposed structures would need to respond to variations of climate and topography, and they would need to respect, but not imitate, the historical and cultural context.

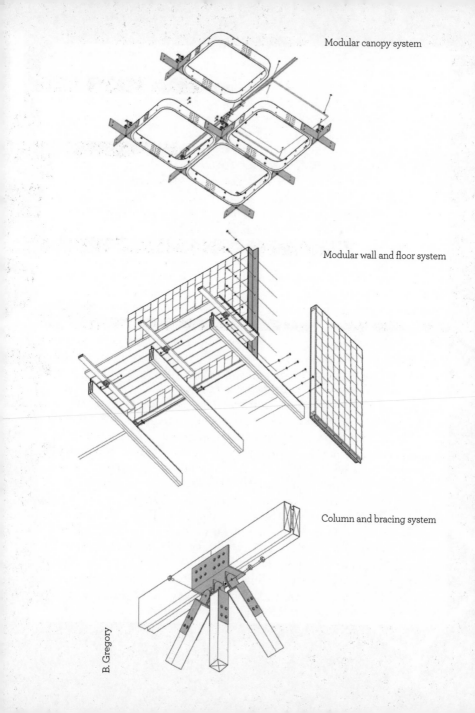

Modular canopy system

Modular wall and floor system

Column and bracing system

B. Gregory

The first exercise is to generate forms from joints drawn from vernacular architecture and architectural history. The structures are similar to buildings but have no functional purpose.

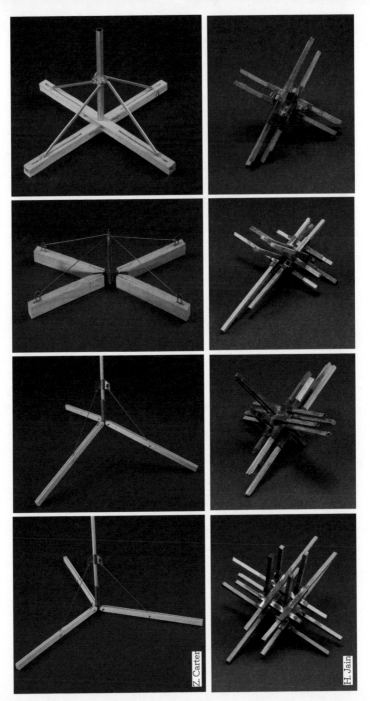

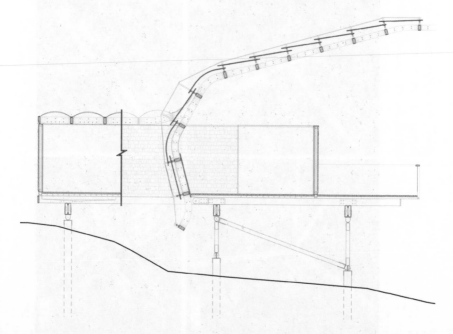

B. Gregory

The design originated with a 4'X4' bent wood box that aggregates to form a versatile two-way grid. This system is able to be disassembled bay-by-bay from the front of the structure and added to the back end, responding to the erosion of the cliff on which the building sits.

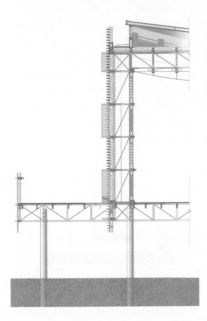

Downeast Southwest

Earl Mark_Spring 2013_Research Studio

Climate change and the need to protect coastlines may cause a paradigm shift in how buildings near oceans are made and occupied. Schoodic Educational Research Center (SERC) at Schoodic Point, located within Acadia National Park in "Down East" Maine, is situated in a dramatic pink granite coastal setting, a place of abundant ocean life, seabirds, powerful waves, undersea fjords, and the mixing of water currents from the Canadian Maritimes and the Gulf of Mexico. Less than ten people live at SERC in winter. During warmer months SERC may lodge three hundred people overnight. During the summer Schoodic Point attracts roughly 250,000 daytime visitors.

Travelling to SERC, this studio designs low-impact, retractable lab space and lodging for educators, visiting scientists, artists, and K-12 students. Students examine the heritage of local wooden-boat building and sail making relevant to tension membrane fabric and lightweight architecture construction.

The primary focus is four retractable lab/residential buildings of one thousand square feet. The small scale provides an opportunity to detail and prototype building components. Each student develops a project thesis that considers his or her design's visual and ecological impact on plants, seabirds and other animals, and the health of the coastline and intertidal areas, and that responds to the potential of a rising ocean level.

Schoodic Point, Maine
Stasis
Generative Detail / Paradigm Shift

Climate change and the need to protect coastlines may cause a paradigm shift in how buildings near oceans are made and occupied.

"The notion of topology has particular potentiality in architecture, as emphasis shifts away from particular forms of expression to relations that exist between and within an existing site and the proposed program. These interdependences then become the structuring, organizing principle for the generation and transformation of form. What makes topology particularly appealing are not the complex forms, such as the Mobius strip, but the primacy over form of the 'structure of relations,' interconnections, or inherent qualities, which exist internally and externally within the context of an architectural project."

(Branko Kolarevic, *Architecture in the Digital Age: Design and Manufacturing*, 2003)

Interdependent Modulation

Parametric Differentiation in Aerospace Architecture

Mara Marcu_Fall 2012_Research Studio

HENRI COANDA AIRPORT TERMINAL 2 Airports are independent—yet, within their own network, interdependent—islands of mythological content defying time, boundaries, and gravity. From the winged deities of the ancient Near East to the angels of the Bible and the winged souls of Plato's *Phaedrus* and throughout Shamanism and Sufism, poets and writers have portrayed flight as a universal symbol of ascension of the human soul to what was thought to be a higher reality. This research studio proposes to understand airports as more than massive infrastructures within an equally intricate economic framework and invites students to showcase imagined possibilities for the Romanian international airport design. While taking cues from local cultural indicators such as the Romanian aviation pioneers Aurel Vlaicu and Henri Coanda, the students are encouraged to take into consideration multilayered factors such as urbanization, globalization, security, materials innovations, adaptability, and travelers' experiences from "curbside to airside." This studio traveled to New York JFK Airport to visit Eero Saarinen's TWA Terminal, which is thought of as a wonderful example of an infrastructure that magically negotiates between all of the above-mentioned elements.

The studio speculates on the possibilities of architectural modulation, made possible through the use of current technologies, which transgresses the benefits of modularity through its capacity for endowing static base units with responsiveness to functional, cultural, and climatic constraints, while retaining a robust system for expansion and modification over time.

Bucharest, Romania
Stasis
Generative Detail / Type

V. Azevedo

Usually situated far away from the cities and with decisive engineering factors taking precedence over any site-related considerations, airports are perhaps one of the only architectural design problems that start off with a blank slate with respect to its site. Although international and generic—therefore not site-specific—airports rely on architectural design to reconcile their engineering and efficiency constraints with the cultural and climatic specifics of the host country. Students are asked to engage in introspective research about airport design within one of the main industrial centers and busiest transportation hubs of Eastern Europe. Bucharest is the capital and the cultural, industrial, and financial center of Romania, officially established in 1459. Its eclectic architecture is a narrative of the country's turbulent history, containing ancient traces of several hundred-years-long wars with the Roman, Ottoman, and Austro-Hungarian Empires and marked by a mix of neoclassical, interbellum (Bauhaus and Art Deco), Communist-era, and modern styles. The programmatic requirements of a new terminal building are mediated within this cultural framework to accommodate a new Departure and Arrivals Hall, a concourse, and access to the future A3 motorway, the railway system, and the future Bucharest Metro Line M6.

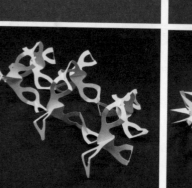

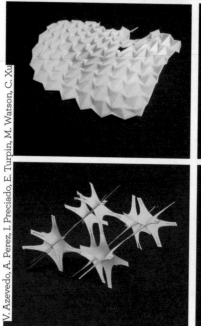

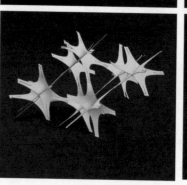

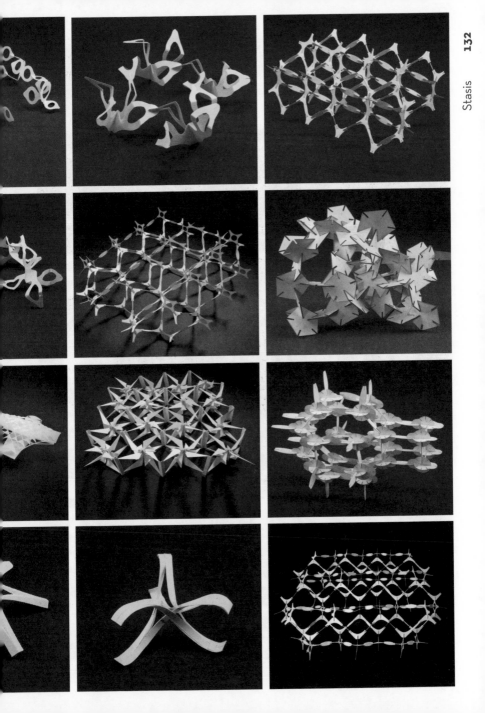

V. Azevedo

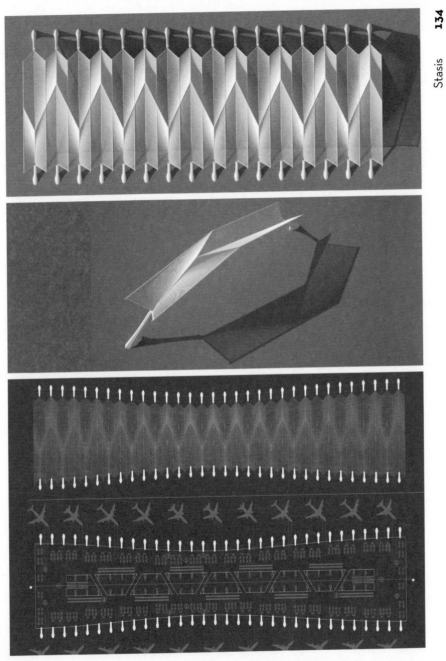

I. Preciado

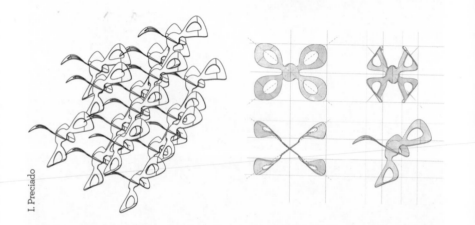

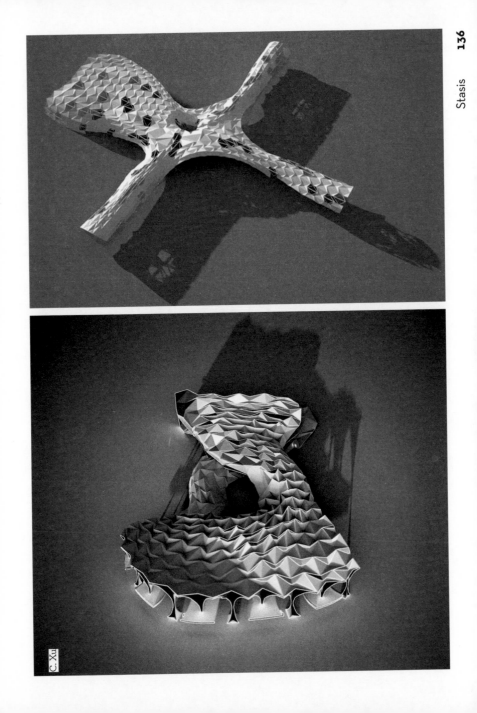

Forms
of Concrete

Alexander Kitchin_Spring 2013_Research Studio

This studio seeks to develop an intuition of material-based design, where the thought and the act of architecture are simultaneous and complementary. The students are asked to understand space, occupation, material, and making by alternating between computer visualization, theoretical positing, and digital and manual making. In this funded research studio we do not only investigate the boundaries of concrete design using all the latest high-tech developments; we also look for an understanding and a new definition of the material and the design process. The research takes place somewhere between the first and the fourth floor of the School, somewhere between the studio and the shop, or more accurately, everywhere in between the head and hands, the space and the surface.

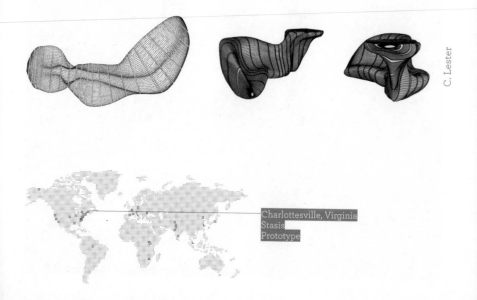

C. Lester

Charlottesville, Virginia
Stasis
Prototype

A. Berndt, P. Brennan, D. Eads, S. Lee, C. Lester, J. Majali, S. Mundy, T. O'Neill, A. Rhees, F. Tai, D. Vejar, M. Wheeler, E. Wilkinson, A. Williams

Wood Manufacturing and Construction Systems

Jeana Ripple_Spring 2013_Research Studio

This studio focuses on regional wood manufacturing and construction systems, analyzing their development in three phases: material, energy, and information. We explore the extent to which information technology can be employed in the further development of wood construction systems using the local production economy as a platform for further innovation. Students conducted a thorough investigation of both contemporary and historical development of wood manufacturing in order to understand the cultural forces shaping material production. They studied wood manufacturing technology through on-site observation at a range of local fabrication and research facilities. The studio operated in three cycles of making, analysis, and contextual research, building a library of material and structural innovations. In the final phase, students developed three prototypes to explore new material efficiencies, reuse potentials, life-cycle optimization, scales of additive manufacturing, and computer numerically controlled (CNC) techniques, along with structural optimization.
The results suggest potential for architects to understand and manipulate details of material production that ultimately influence design limitations and opportunities at every scale.

[siteless]
Stasis
Prototype

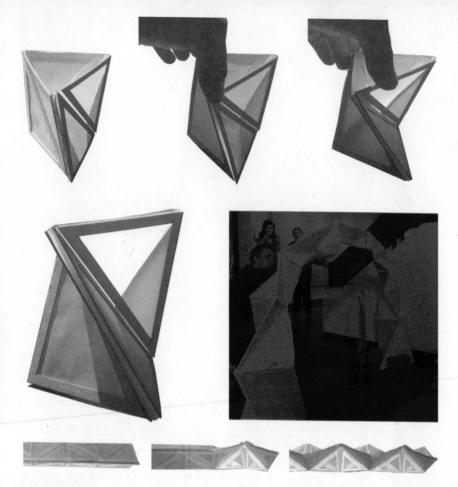

Modular Tensegrity

William Artrip, Joy Hu, Kathleen Lavelle, Valeria Rivera (further analysis completed by Joy Hu and Ryan Metcalf as part of Jeana Ripple's "Structuring Logic" seminar)

Beginning with an interest in dual-purpose engineered wood products (such as SIPs panels), this project explored the potential for common construction materials to work in combination for greater structural performance. Inspired by the efficiency and resiliency of tensegrity structures, a hybrid structural system of rigid panels and flexible joints was developed, utilizing OSB and HDPE building wrap. But unlike the traditionally pure strut-and-cable tensegrity systems, parametric and physical models were used to understand and vary the size and orientation of the module, while preserving its ability to aggregate and lock into place as a self-supporting system. The system integrated flexibility and structure, utilizing two materials that are typically understood as independent systems. It is easily manufactured off-site, flat-packed, and then expanded and assembled on-site. The final arch reveals one method of aggregation and proposes future possibilities of this hybrid modular unit.

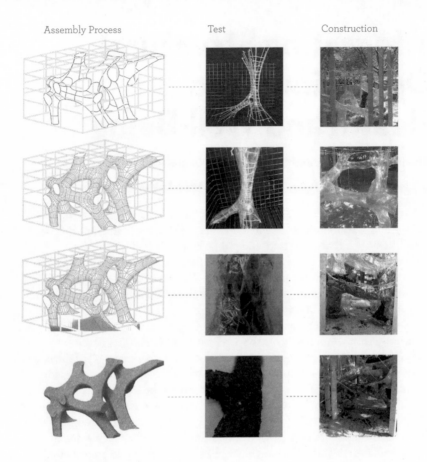

Assembly Process   Test   Construction

Trabecular Sculptacular

Roderick Cruz, Jenny Fang, Han Jin, Allen Merced, Tae Park, Michael Stanley

3-D printing is heralded as the future of manufacturing. Researchers are testing diverse possibilities ranging from wood-based filament to large-scale machines. However, critics claim that limitations in speed, cost, and size will never catch up to the efficiencies of more traditional repetitive manufacturing processes. With this in mind, this project explores the greatest inherent strength in 3-D printing technology: increased complexity equals lower cost (less material). Focusing on systems where complexity creates a particular advantage, a parametric modeling method was developed to approximate human trabecular bone structure, a natural model for simultaneous strength and efficiency. A new filament was explored at a coarse scale of resolution for faster, larger-scale production, utilizing the largest wood-waste product in current production cycles: tree bark. Our physical modeling tested the limitations of the filament, aggregate, and binding agent to branch at an angle and still support its own weight. This process ultimately resulted in producing an algorithm for the future of large-scale wood 3-D printing, utilizing the true efficiency of this technology and minimizing the amount of secondary support.

Integrating Structural Operations into Health and Well-Being

Gravity, Orientation, and the Pursuit of Happiness

Schaeffer Somers + Peter Waldman_Fall 2012_Research Studio

This studio is an ongoing dialogue between two instructors, Peter Waldman and Schaeffer Somers. The research agenda emerges from the intersection of architecture, urban planning, and public health, framing the built environment as a complex system that has direct impacts on human health. It seeks to address these questions: *What are the measures of health, happiness, and well-being in a human population? How does a building shape the health of its inhabitants and the community at large? What are the parameters of a livable, equitable, and prosperous urban ecology?*

Beginning with an intense workshop in Structural Operations, students integrate material, structure, and building code into parametric and physical models of stairs and pedestrian bridges as key programmatic elements in promoting physical activity. The studio introduces didactic topics including visual-impairments mobility, neighborhood completeness, walkability, age-friendly cities, and barrier-free design. Logic modeling is imported from public health sciences as a tool for diagramming causal relationships in evidence-based design. Working in teams, students propose projects that incorporate the programmatic requirements of a range of clients from the health sciences community.

The territory of the studio is the gradient from University Avenue to the auto-centric commercial highway US 29. The projects are networked through mobility systems and other urban ecologies.

Charlottesville, Virginia
Stasis
System

D. Eads

Drawing upon a lifetime of teaching culminating in the course "Lessons of the Lawn," Peter challenges the students to go beyond evidence and logic with the following prompt:

"Can the sensibilities of Surveyors, Nomads, or Lunatics (those who contemplate the myriad phases of the Moon) also articulate the characteristics of this extensive site and distinct programs yielding well-being in a newly explored Common Ground? There is a cast of characters, key informants and community partners who will contribute their expertise. Each stakeholder may represent distinct orientations with thresholds juxtaposed to enter, four windows to look out, and finally four more to look within as sunset yields to darkness. Some may excavate deep basements, while others map the skies by day and by night. Each institution may exist as a world unto itself, but may also map, envision, perhaps approximate (as an asymptote) a meditative pause between the visceral ground and the ethereal sky. These institutions of health and well-being are as distinct as Water, Fire, Earth, and Air, but they all may claim the peace of the ethereal as well-being with the World. As the Academical Village and Monticello are both lifelong projects, this "real project" aspires to making several centers, fragmentary frames, and spatial leaks, if not moments to trespass. We will imagine another vision of "A City on a Hill," a recurrent dream in world culture of an Other paradise, an Other new beginning."

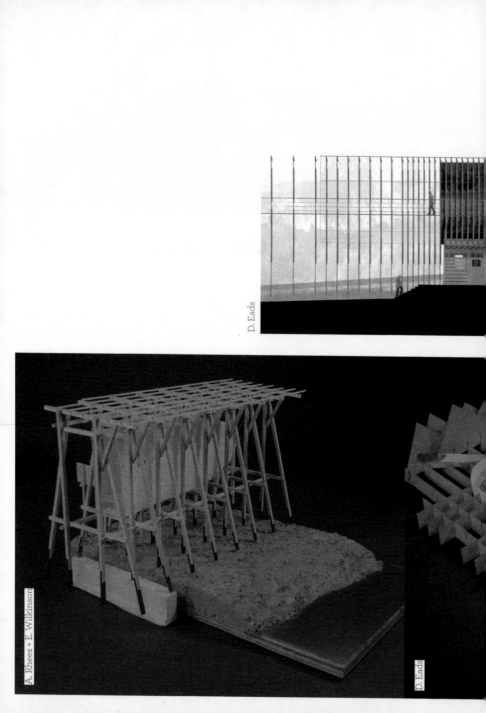

A. Rhees + E. Wilkinson

D. Eads

D. Eads

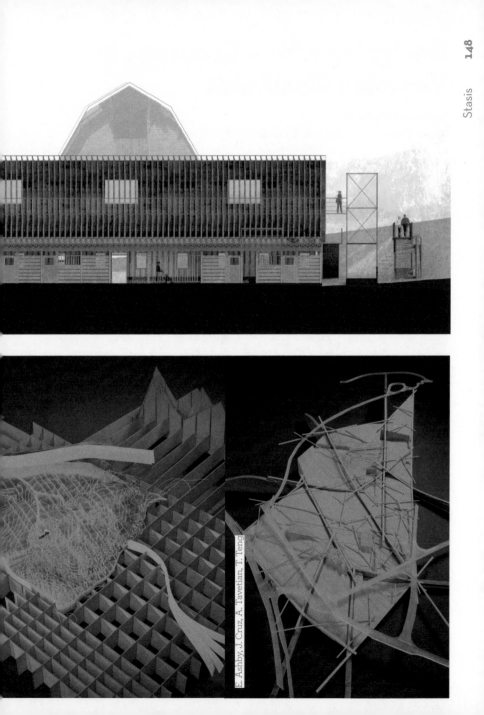

E. Ashby, J. Cruz, A. Tavetian, T. Teng

Designing a New Economy in Virginia's Coalfields

Suzanne Moomaw
Department of Urban and Environmental Planning

Cities, communities, and small towns are dealing with a changing economy and a global manufacturing and distribution system that is no longer place-bound, and cities themselves—not nation-states—are at the nexus of these changes. As Parag Khanna wrote in *Foreign Policy* (September/October 2010), "The future world order and the economy that supports it will be built on cities." While most attention and emphasis is given to global cities like London, New York, and Paris, and financial hubs such as Shanghai, Sydney, Hong Kong, and Tokyo, smaller municipalities in the United States and around the world must act and react in these new economic conditions as well. The consequences have been particularly adverse for those with mature industries. Some of the hardest hit areas are in the industrial Midwest and Northeast, where agriculture, low-skill manufacturing sectors such as textiles, and extractive industries have long predominated.

Several applied courses in both Architecture and Urban and Environmental Planning are addressing ways to increase the competitiveness of such communities and to improve their quality of life through better and expanded housing, healthcare, and living-wage jobs in the towns and cities most affected by the new realities of global capitalism. One partner community is the southwest Virginia town of Appalachia, which has a population of about two thousand people. Founded in 1908, the downtown area boomed as the demand for coal grew across the country. As machines began to replace men in the mines and as global demand began to fall, however, Appalachia experienced a major economic downturn. Today mining remains a major source of employment but the numbers are declining. As evidence of the long tradition, nine historic coal camps radiate from the town of Appalachia, including Andover, Arno, Derby, Roda, Imboden, Exeter, Dunbar, Pardee, Osaka, and Stonega.[1] Coal companies owned the camp housing and all the amenities within it. This situation was neither novel nor unique. As the Industrial Revolution took hold in America in the nineteenth century, rows of similar, if not identical, company houses were built outside factories, lumberyards, coal-mines, and textile mills. Volumes have been written about life in mill villages. In these planned camps, the community was experienced as something more than housing stock. People worked, worshiped, and socialized together.

The company towns often had their own schools, stores, churches, boarding houses, and parks. Workers made a decent wage and that money either stayed in the camp or permeated into the primary community; this was the case in the camps surrounding Appalachia. Times have changed, however. With a poverty rate of 28 percent for families and an average household income of $20,405, the area is facing many economic challenges. Not least among them is how to build a new economy on an old footprint, how to foster opportunities for entrepreneurial development, and how to retain young people and prepare them for twenty-first-century jobs. However, despite the challenges the town has many assets, among them the George Washington Natural Forest, which is a gateway to a range of recreational opportunities. The town boasts one of the most complete model railroad displays in the state and has very distinctive architecture. Through a partnership with communities and agencies in the coal region of southwestern Virginia, students and faculty are working with the town of Appalachia to develop a new strategy for economic and community development through the Community Design and Research Center and our university partner, the Appalachian Prosperity Project.

In 2012-13, thirty students and three faculty members worked with town leaders in Appalachia to research and help implement plans that could bring more tourists, more jobs, and more visibility to the area. Collaborative teams of architectural, planning, historic preservation, and landscape students have pursued a range of projects driven by the town's interests. These include conceiving a new Rails-to-Trails project, a digital visualization of the trail that corresponds to the requirements of the Americans with Disabilities Act, signage that highlights the natural habitat, the mapping of cultural and historical resources to support a cultural tourism initiative, a new town website, and informational brochures that have helped the town brand and market itself more effectively around its coal, railroad, and recreational history.

[1] http://en.wikipedia.org/wiki/Appalachia,_Virginia

A proposed design to connect the new Rails-to-Trails project with Riverside Park. This was developed during a postgraduate trip of Appalachian Prosperity Project Fellows from Architecture, Landscape Architecture, and Urban and Environmental Planning. Three route options are proposed, each with slightly different relationships to the river, roads, and rail line.

UVa Design Office

Margarita Jover and UVa School of Architecture

The Design Office is a new institution at the University of Virginia School of Architecture that was established at the beginning of the fall 2012 semester as a pilot program lead by Margarita Jover, Architect, Lecturer, and Principal at aldayjover Architecture & Landscape. The UVa Design Office is intended to link and serve from a design perspective the different research and pedagogical agendas of the School and the University as well as the larger community. The Design Office is open to all faculty, students, and staff of the School. It will provide them the opportunity to participate in design projects addressing topics generated inside and outside the School, and will establish partnership among the many disciplines of the school, as well as the wider academic community at UVa. The Office offers applied design and planning research resources to the School, the University, the City of Charlottesville, and the Society, without interfering or competing with the practicing professionals, but creating opportunities for partnership.

Project 1:

During the fall 2012 semester, Margarita Jover, with three dual-degree students—Aja Bulla-Richards (MArch'13-MLA'13), Jack Cochran (MArch'13-MUEP'13), and Kurt Marsh (MArch'13-MLA'13)—proposed a new public space structure for the Central Grounds of the University of Virginia. The proposal was displayed on three urban entities at different scales called: the RING^C, the WALK^C and the BRIDGE^C.

The RING^C is a proposed urban entity that includes a track of bikes inserted safely within a planted boulevard that transforms the current nexus of Preston Avenue, McIntire Road, West Main Street, Jefferson Park Avenue, Emmet Street, and Barracks Road into an intermodal urban street. Bikes, cars, and two types of buses navigate around the ring that produce an understanding

RING´s schematic plan (green) at the city

of the City and the University as a whole, compact, and well-connected urban body with intermodal stations located near parking structures, buildings and bus and bike stations, which enable the easy alternation between one mode of transportation and another. In addition, the RING^c is also conceived as an urban entity that can be densely urbanized in the future with housing, commerce, offices as well as green open spaces.

The WALK^c is the second urban entity, proposed for McCormick Road, the main purpose of which is to recover the sense of safety and urbanity on Central Grounds. Drawing on the culture and history of the site, these proposed open-door spaces could be given such names as Edgar Allen Poe Square, Monroe Square, or DuBois Square and establish relations of complicity within buildings that

WALK´s schematic plan at central grounds.

surround them. This proposed WALK^c aims to recover the sense of urbanity rebalancing the automobile's supremacy with the proposed intermodality of the RING^c.

Finally, the third urban entity, smaller in scale is The BRIDGE^c, which is a new bridge-square over Emmet Street. The BRIDGE^c would expand across a large surface, with an opening for light, as well as an elevator that connects

an important intermodal site below— bikes and buses—with the upper level where proposed cafés and the like could improve the dynamism and vitality of the surrounding area. The structure is comprised of a series of prestressed concrete beams re-covered with wood, stainless steel, and glass.

BRIDGE's plan over Emmet street

Project 2: In the spring 2013 semester, with Rebecca Hora (MArch'13) and Mariam Rahmatullah (BSArch'13), the Design Office proposed a new addition to the Fiske Kimball Fine Arts Library, as well as a reorganization of the Library as an institution connected in new and different ways to Central Grounds and Arts Grounds. In addition, it has been proposed that the Music Department should relocate from Old Cabell Hall to a space near the library. The proposal was displayed on three areas at different scale called the OUTDOOR, the INDOOR, and the INSTITUTION.

The OUTDOOR is a proposed revitalization of the pos of the Arts Grounds within Central Grounds. A Boulevard of the Arts is proposed at Rugby Road with three clear, stair-free pedestrian means of access to the library where civility would be improved while preserving some of the wildness of the landscape.

The INDOOR is a proposal that addresses the lack of natural light, elevators, stairs, restrooms, offices, and book storage. It also seeks to cultivate a more dynamic interaction with the School of Architecture, the Fine Arts Café, and Ruffin Hall. The spaces are organized in three categories according to noise level.

Finally, the INSTITUTION is a proposal to organize the building as a Cultural Center that includes the Fiske Kimball Fine Arts Library. The Institution would be situated within different departments and Schools that could interact easily in the proposed new gallery spaces near the lecture halls. The Institution could provide a venue for theater for kids, debates, discussions, expositions, gallery talks, or musical performances, supported by a variety of creative funding mechanisms.

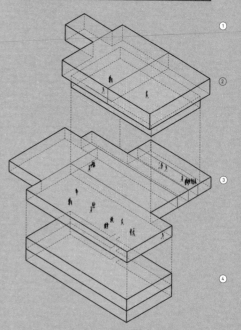

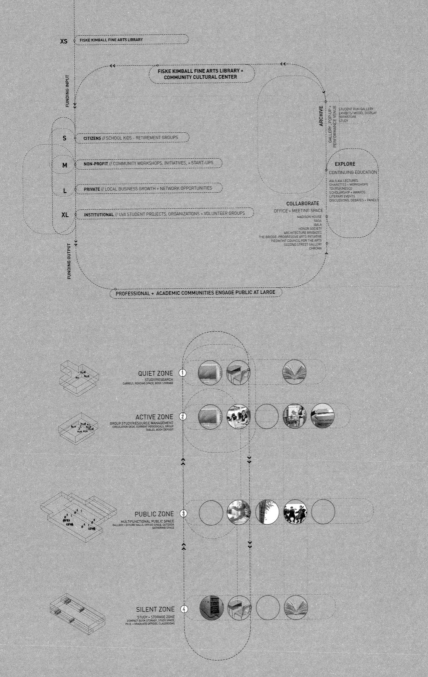

XS FISKE KIMBALL FINE ARTS LIBRARY

FUNDING INPUT

FISKE KIMBALL FINE ARTS LIBRARY +
COMMUNITY CULTURAL CENTER

ARCHIVE

STUDENT RUN GALLERY
EXHIBITS/ MODEL DISPLAY
BOOKSTORE
STUDY

GALLERY · POP-UP ·
PERFORMANCE VENUE

S CITIZENS // SCHOOL KIDS - RETIREMENT GROUPS

M NON-PROFIT // COMMUNITY WORKSHOPS, INITIATIVES, + START-UPS

L PRIVATE // LOCAL BUSINESS GROWTH + NETWORK OPPORTUNITIES

XL INSTITUTIONAL // UVA STUDENT PROJECTS, ORGANIZATIONS + VOLUNTEER GROUPS

EXPLORE

CONTINUING EDUCATION

AIA /\ AIA LECTURES
CHARETTES + WORKSHOPS
TOUR/UNESCO
SCHOLARSHIP + AWARDS
LITERARY EVENTS
DISCUSSIONS, DEBATES + PANELS

COLLABORATE

OFFICE + MEETING SPACE

MADISON HOUSE
SABA
GALA
HONOR SOCIETY
ARCHITECTURE BRIGADES
THE BRIDGE- PROGRESSIVE ARTS INITIATIVE
PIEDMONT COUNCIL FOR THE ARTS
SECOND STREET GALLERY
CHROMA

FUNDING OUTPUT

PROFESSIONAL + ACADEMIC COMMUNITIES ENGAGE PUBLIC AT LARGE

QUIET ZONE

STUDY/RESEARCH
CARRELS, READING SPACE, BOOK STORAGE

①

ACTIVE ZONE

GROUP STUDY/RESOURCE MANAGEMENT
CIRCULATION DESK, CURRENT PERIODICALS, GROUP
TABLES, BOOK DEPOSIT

②

PUBLIC ZONE

MULTIFUNCTIONAL PUBLIC SPACE
GALLERY, LECTURE HALLS, OFFICE SPACE, OUTDOOR
GATHERING SPACE

③

SILENT ZONE

STUDY + STORAGE ZONE
COMPACT BOOK STORAGE, STUDY SPACE,
PH.D. + GRADUATE OFFICES, CLASSROOMS

④

Expanding Eruv

Semiotics, Infrastructure, and the Making of Jewish Space

Isaac Cohen, MLA 2013 + Isaac Hametz, MLA 2013 + Rae Vassar, MLA 2014
Benjamin C. Howland Fellowship

The research presented here tests sociospatial theories through primary field research conducted on the Jewish practice of *eruv*. Synthesizing a combination of participatory observation, primary-source text analysis, and field documentation, this project presents and describes a methodology for decoding spatial production and the urban invisible. Translated literally, *eruv* means "mixture," "involvement," or "partnership." In practice, however, eruv is a physically constructed Rabbinic infrastructure that utilizes elements of the city, both civic and structural, to define public and private spatial domains on the Sabbath for purposes of Jewish ritual observance. This investigation questions how urban theorists and designers view and represent the urban invisible and how processes of spatial production in the city contribute to, modify, and/or alleviate social inequality. As a point of entry into a larger discussion of socially produced space and self-conscious human action, eruv is a useful paradigm. The complex and often messy interaction of space and time that occurs in the realm of the urban requires concrete examples that challenge and test contemporary theories. By engaging the specificities of eruv practice in the context of a discussion of socially produced space, it is possible to suggest a hybrid condition of spatial control that offers an alternative to oppositional binaries and monofunctional infrastructures.

Perceived Space

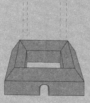

Conceived Space

Lived Space

West Rogers Park Eruv · Chicago, IL

Contemplative Spaces

Advanced GIS

Guoping Huang _Spring 2013

The new UVA Contemplative Sciences Center (CSC) aims to create an inventory of the best contemplative spaces on Grounds. Ideally, the Center wants a searchable, web-based platform that would identify desirable locations based on the spatial attributes necessary for the intended type of practice. Students built a geodatabase of all the indoor and outdoor spaces on Grounds with GIS data and floor plans from the Office of the Architect. They focused on producing detailed spatial attributes for a subset of five outdoor locations and thirty rooms. They then analyzed the spatial attributes of these spaces based on the spatial, temporal, and acoustic requirements of contemplative practices. ArcGIS Model Builder was used to perform suitability analysis in order to find the ideal spaces for different types of contemplation, such as meditation, yoga, tai chi, etc. A user is able to pick a combination of criteria and weigh them to find the ideal space in the geospatial inventory.

The procedures and outputs of this project provide a starting point for the Contemplative Sciences Center, and with further development will become a useful resource for a variety of contemplative practitioners.

Vegetation

Rooms + Topography

Solar radiation (Fall afternoon)

Noise level (Rush Hour)

Students: Margot Elton, Abbey Ness, Wendy Phelps, Matthew West, and Chelsea Zhou
3DUVA: UVA central grounds in 3D (Basemap provided by the Office of Architect)

Site/Sound

Karen Van Lengen with IATH and Partners_2013

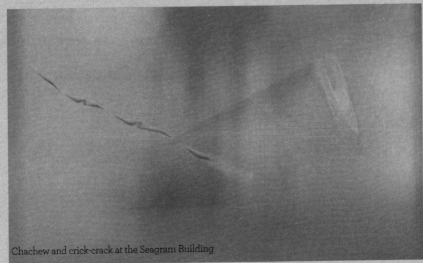

Chachew and crick-crack at the Seagram Building

The Site/Sounds Project is a web-based analytical and perceptual learning environment that demonstrates the synthetic relation between the visual, auditory, and material aspects of architectural space. The website includes analytical and interpretive visualizations as well as new sound compositions, all based on actual sound recordings of iconic architectural spaces. For example, the Seagram Building's all glass lobby captures both the general acoustical landscape of this vibrant lobby while also featuring a range of highly specific sounds that amplify its mystique as a prominent gateway to an architectural landmark.

2.4 Squeaky Wheel

4.7, 6.1 Little Clang

8.8 Big Clang

18.2 Shake Shake

33 Little Clang

39, 42, 46 Clang

47, 48 Castanet

55 Second Castanet

"In the process of comparing and superimposing individual forms so as to determine the type, particular characteristics of each individual building are eliminated and only those remain which are common to every unit of the series. The type therefore, is formed through a process of reducing a complex of formal variants to a common root form. [The type] has to be understood as the interior structure of a form or as a principle which contains the possibility of infinite formal variation and further structural modification of the type itself."

(Argan, "On Typology of Architecture," 1963)

"The definition of type that we have tried to propose for urban artifacts and architecture, a definition which was first enunciated in the Enlightenment, allows us to proceed to an accurate classification of urban artifacts, and ultimately also to a classification based on function wherever the latter constitutes an aspect of the general definition. If, alternatively, we begin with a classification based on function, type would have to be treated in a very different way; indeed, if we insist on the primacy of function we must then understand type as the organizing model of this function. But this understanding of type, and consequently urban artifacts and architecture, as the organizing principle of certain functions, almost totally denies us an adequate knowledge of reality. Even if a classification of buildings and cities according to their function is permissible as a generalization of certain kinds of data, it is inconceivable to reduce the structure of urban artifacts to a problem of organizing some more or less important function. Precisely this serious distortion has impeded and in large measure continues to impede any real progress in studies of the city." (Rossi, *The Architecture of the City*, 1982)

"Among the difficulties posed by type—a concept that has replaced the anxiety of originality with the anxiety of origin—is the decision concerning the criteria that must be present to allow the recognition of a legitimate type form, against which the similar, the almost, and the barely recognizable will always be in varying stages of revolt. The 'proper' manifestation of type develops the notion of an orthodoxy that is in essence inimical to architectural manipulation and to the specificity of a building as opposed to 'building.' Such an orthodoxy stands mute in instances of hybridization, where typologies of form must give way to typologies of operation." (Graf, "Diagrams," 1986)

An Institute for Materials Research

Shiqiao Li_Spring 2013_Research Studio

We seem to relate to materials in three ways: economically, experientially, and artistically. We tend to stress experiential and artistic relationships to materials in design, and deservingly so, as they are fundamental to the human psyche and intellect, understood through science, phenomenology, and critical theory. The economic relationship to materials, on the other hand, is much less discussed in relation to design.

We live at a time when the economic relationship with materials is monopolized by global capital; through the division of labor, return on investment, spatial and temporal displacement of capital, all materials production seems to have become profit oriented, which returns in the form of goods of convenience and fast deterioration. The debasement of the economic relationship to materials, as a kind of alienation, becomes the debasement of the experiential connection.

This Institute of Materials Research aims to work simultaneously with three material possibilities: economy, experience, and art. Programmatically, it contains a goods workshop, a school of craft, and a resident artist studio. By merging all three into one single entity, this Institute aims to demonstrate the full potential of materials and to advance a new economic life which attempts to redress the distorting and alienating effects of capital on human life and the equitable rights of things in the environment.

Charlottesville, Virginia
Stasis
Type

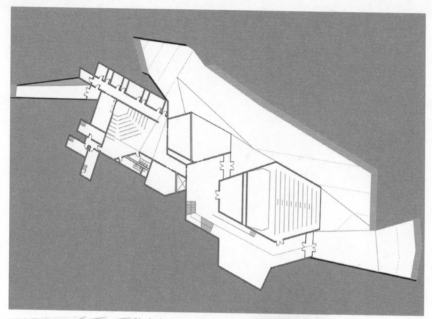

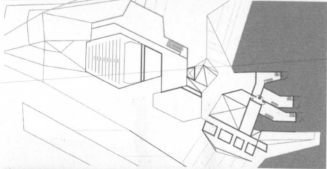

Material study: ceramics - C. Chu + I. Kim, sound - M. Watson, wind - R. Grooms + J. Moore + M. Morales

By merging all three possibilities—economy, experience, and art—into a single entity, this Institute aims to demonstrate the full potential of materials and to advance a new economic life which attempts to redress the distorting and alienating effects of capital on human life and the equitable rights of things in the environment.

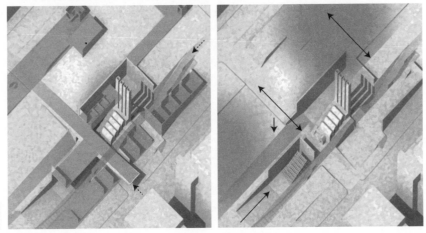

I. Kim

Community and Privacy

W.G. Clark_Spring 2013_Foundation Studio

This project comprises two programs of an almost opposite nature: one is a community center, the heart of its social neighborhood; the other is private housing.

A big component of the community center is child care for working parents: all-day care for young children and after-school care for grade-schoolers and teens where they are offered a safe, structured environment for homework and activities. Adults, including the elderly, enjoy theater, dance, yoga, swimming, arts and crafts, cooking lessons, films, and lectures. There are also weekend activities like community dinners, music events, and tours to other places.

In order to help subsidize the center, a number of apartments of varying sizes are included in the program. The City imagines around two dozen, but recognizes that the specific site chosen might limit the number.

There are a variety of sites, mostly vacant lots, from which students choose. After selecting one (or two, for comparative studies) students document it and its immediate context with measurement, photography, and research of its history. The specific program is of the student's own design. Suggestions are offered, but the principal goal is for the student to imagine what a new community center could be, what it might include and what form it might take. Then, together, the studio produces a program that serves that vision.

Philadelphia, Pennsylvania
Stasis
Type

R. Carbone

The project serves one of the earliest settled
areas along the Delaware River, Old City, and its
neighboring area, Northern Liberties in Philadelphia.
Both sectors were filled with manufacturing and
stores from the early 1800s until the industries
moved west and the Benjamin Franklin Bridge
divided them. The area deteriorated and was largely
vacant through the 1960s when developers retrofitted
the warehouses as apartments. The transformation
of Old City spread to Northern Liberties and to
Fishtown beyond.

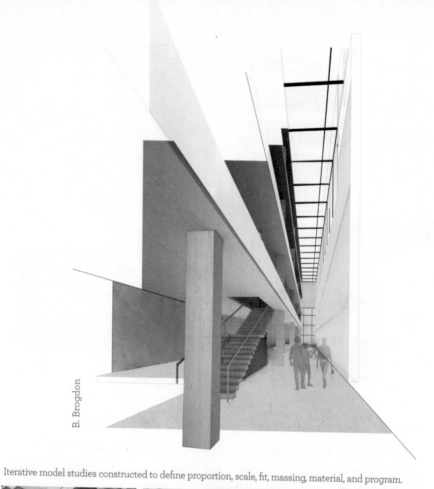

B. Brogdon

Iterative model studies constructed to define proportion, scale, fit, massing, material, and program.

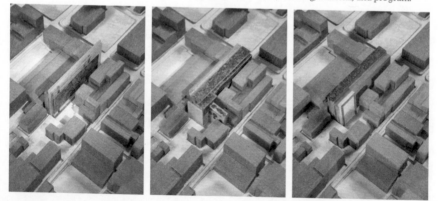

Designing in Place

Prospects for a Contemporary, Rooted, Everyday Architecture

Jesse Wilks, M.Arch 2013_Thesis
Advisor: W.G. Clark

Designing in Place seeks to generate an improved everyday built environment by establishing a design process driven by ethics rather than form making. Its goal is to create contemporary, economical architecture that is sensitive to site and place, contributes to an ongoing building culture, and celebrates the most ordinary human activities.

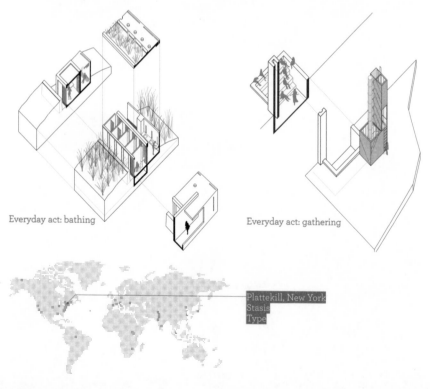

Everyday act: bathing

Everyday act: gathering

Plattekill, New York
Stasis
Type

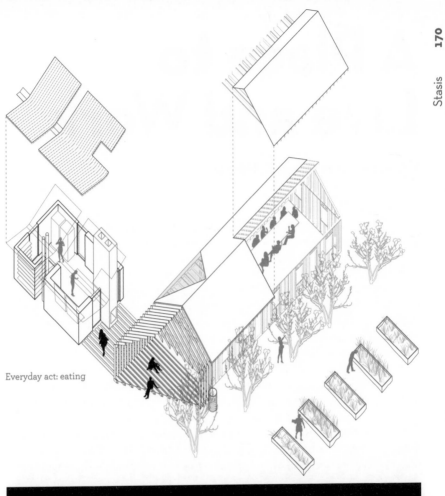

Everyday act: eating

A Place to Live and Work

W.G. Clark_Fall 2012_Research Studio

The subject of this project is an urban house for two people. It is a small project for several reasons, including aesthetic intensity and a wish to demonstrate that resolution and detailing are critical to design intentions. There are encouraging trends related to houses in this country. One is that people have started returning to cities. The suburbs are unsustainable for both infrastructure and travel. They can't offer the vitality and sense of community that urban settlement can. This trend may profoundly color the larger landscape. Another trend—people are beginning to work at home instead of commuting—invites new ways of thinking about dwelling and how it may be integral to both work and creation.

So with these things in mind this project begins with several vacant lots in Charlottesville. Each is an intense location responsible to civic context as well as to the privacy of the couple living within. The first act of design is choosing the site; the second is understanding its history and physical properties. While doing so students also imagine their clients and their work, allowing them to define a program of spaces and their qualities and contents. Our method of study and design concentrates on physical modeling and on multiple iterations or permutations of each. Students make several models a week, stressing the craft of these artifacts, and utilize digital modeling where necessary.

Charlottesville, Virginia
Stasis
Type

V. Badami

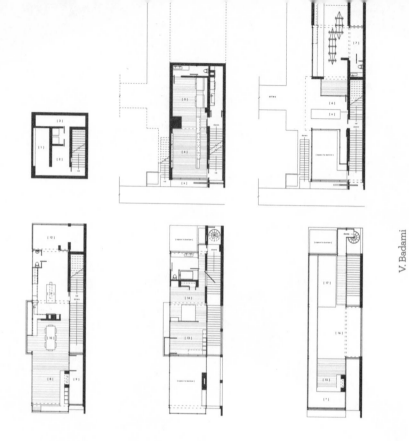

V. Badami

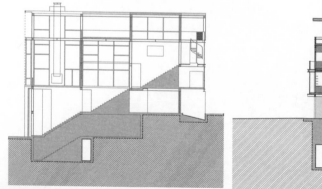

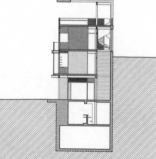

A. Cellar
B. Wine Shop
C. Canoe Shop
D. Living Space
E. Mezzanine
F. Roof Terrace

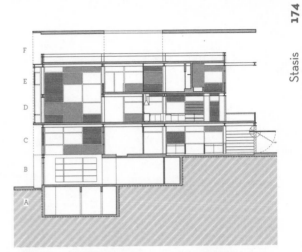

M. Rahmatullah

"The concept of type is in itself open to change insofar as it means a consciousness of actual facts, including, certainly, a recognition of the possibility of change. By looking at architectural objects as groups, as types, susceptible to differentiation in their secondary aspects, the partial obsolescences appearing in them can be appraised, and consequently one can act to change them. The type can thus be thought of as the frame within which change operates, a necessary term to continuing dialectic required by history. From this point of view, the type, rather than being a 'frozen mechanism' to produce architecture, becomes a way of denying the past, as well as a way of looking at the future." (Rafael Moneo, "On Typology," 1978)

Urban Culinary Institute

Peter Waldman_Spring 2013_Foundation Studio

Cast of Characters: A Butcher, a Baker, a Candlestick Maker, and Twenty-eight or Twenty-nine Apprentices

The Institute teaches classes by day and provides feasting halls by night. The Institute has many doors, but few windows. There should be distinct portals for daytime class as well as evening dinners; the journey to their destinations should whet their appetites. Exiting may be a substitute for dessert. You should find yourself somewhere else after all that time and effort. The Institute is a public entity in a merit-based culture. Shortly after Calvino's death—or was it Widow Carr's passing?—a state competition selected three young masters of their crafts to have lifetime tenure to explore lightness and multiplicity. That was some time ago. Recently the Slow Food Institute has proposed a permanent location for these culinary legends at the height of their vigorous maturity. The three wish to dwell on-site and to share a south-facing terrace joining their three laconic cells: each with two doors (one for going in, the other for going out) and only one window (one facing east, a second facing west, the third facing north).

There are twenty-eight (some say twenty-nine) apprentices who train by day and serve by night. They live off-site, need lockers, and are rumored to skateboard home since the vaporetto closes down at midnight.

The kitchen for the school and the feast halls are the same but face two different directions. Service lifts should accommodate routine deliveries from the Pescheria as well as quail eggs from on-site rookeries. Garbage is constant. Drains are everywhere; the entire building is scrubbed down with the regularity of the tides. It is rumored that since Phoenician times, the people of Venice as well as the Piedmont have delighted in three spatially distinct feasting halls: the grotto hidden within a hearth (Torcello & Monticello), the generic celebratory *piano nobile*, and the roof terrace (*altana*). All should be accessible here as determined by season as well as by reason.

various sites: Philadelphia, Pennsylvania New York City, New York Berlin, Germany, etc.

Stasis Type

G. Yu

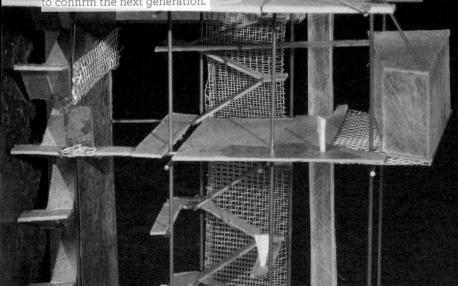

Three institutional laboratories are dedicated to each maestro: one for butchering milk-fed calves as well as an occasional Chingale alongside the culinary consequences of a Spritz Bar on the street level, one for baking and a small retail shop on a garden court, and finally the studio of the candlestick maker facing the best place to catch the setting sun. Stairs are everywhere. The maestros keep trim bustling from attic to basement; some say there are countless secret stairs, others go on and on about the grandest promenade— or is it a conveyor belt?—since Napoleon cut the Strada Nuova. Hydraulic elevators indulge the gourmands and anticipate the return of Marcella Hazan to confirm the next generation.

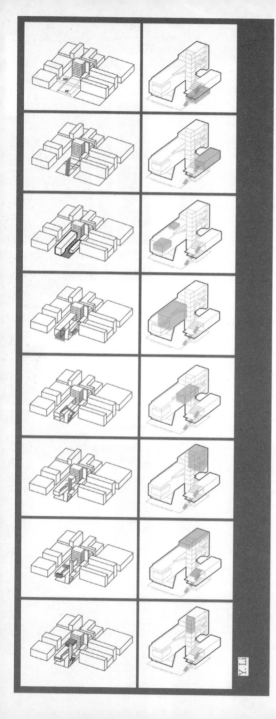

Y. Li

E. Charpentier

The Culinary Institute is located between two Schinkel buildings in Berlin's medieval core. The structure comes together from the fragments of the city, dug out of the ground and put together with rubble and bits and pieces of dismissed buildings.

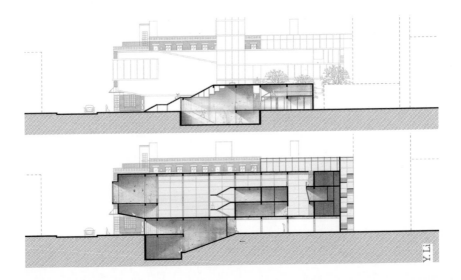

Green Infrastructure as Public Space

The City Market as Social and Ecological Catalyst: Tactical Urbanism, Regional Networks, and Spatial Practices between Farm and Table

Leena Cho + Elizabeth Meyer_Fall 2012_Research Studio

"I recently heard someone remark that farmers markets are a 'Community Living Room,' and I couldn't agree more."
Charlottesville Market Central Newsletter (Fall 2009)

"Urban revitalization practitioners ... understand that public gathering places are inextricably related to the potential for economic opportunity and upward mobility of lower-income people. One of the most obvious, but perhaps least understood, methods of enhancing social integration in public spaces and encouraging upward mobility are public markets." *Public Markets as a Vehicle for Social Integration and Upward Mobility,* Ford Foundation

"The form of social space is encounter, assembly, simultaneity.... The history of space does not have to choose between 'processes' and 'structures,' change and invariability, events and institutions.... The departure point for this history of space is ... in the study of natural rhythms, and of the modifications of those rhythms and their inscription of space by means of human actions, especially work-related actions. It begins, then, with the spatio-temporal rhythms of nature as transformed by a social practice."
Henri Lefebvre, *The Production of Space* (1991).

Charlottesville, Virginia
Stasis
Type

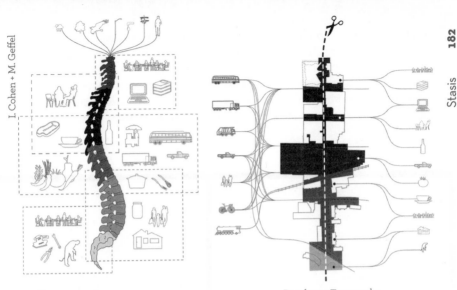

Backbone Network   Regulatory Topography

This vertical studio invited second-and third-year landscape architecture graduate students to select a new site, propose a new vision, and develop design details for the Charlottesville City Market, a seasonal enterprise that takes place on a steep, unsheltered city parking lot. The students were asked to accommodate, expand, and critique the activities and events that currently occur. To this end, the class explored proposals that altered the network of existing public spaces, increased connectivity between the neighborhoods surrounding downtown, catalyzed mixed-use developments with affordable and market-rate housing, improved the ecological performance of the urban landscape infrastructure, and hosted other public functions and events when the market is not open. They developed prototypes for Charlottesville's nascent green infrastructure initiatives and explored the potential for a new market district, which had been suggested in 2011 by David O'Neill, a consultant hired by Market Central, a friends group. City officials and citizens involved in the debates and discussion about the market's future advised the studio and attended reviews. The studio's work included a tactical urbanism invention deploying small-scale landscape elements and spaces to create big impacts; a comparative analysis of markets across the globe; an examination of the relationship between the market, urban networks, local food systems, and regional actors; and the synthesis of that design research into a memorable landscape that incorporated experience, material assembly, events, functional logistics, urban form, and landscape change.

These ideas were examined on-site, from Lee Park and the Downtown Mall to Garrett Street and Monticello Avenue. These distinct sites gave rise to diverse strategies: markets along streets, in plazas, within groves and under shelter; market centers in new residential districts; market retrofits to the Downtown Mall and Lee Park; water markets within waterhoods; and landscape appropriations of existing parking garages as temporary market-event spaces.

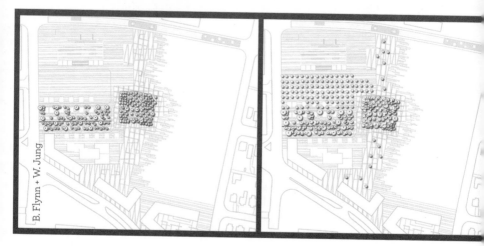

B. Flynn + W. Jung

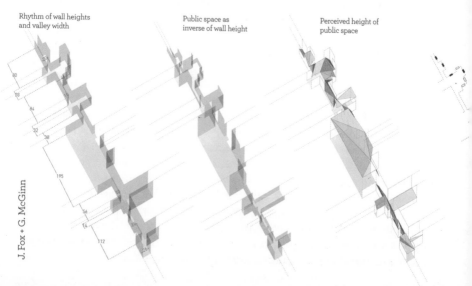

Rhythm of wall heights and valley width

Public space as inverse of wall height

Perceived height of public space

J. Fox + G. McGinn

The studio findings were shared with Market Central, the City's Economic Development and Neighborhood Planning Services staffs, and members of City Council, and as a result a new site is being considered as one of the alternatives for the future market. Deliberations about the market's future site continue...

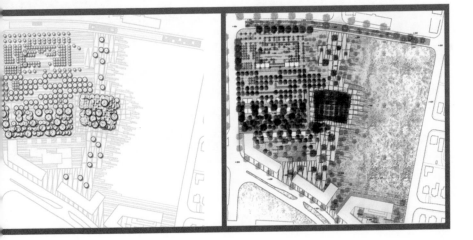

Customer and service entrances

Pedestrian and shared surfaces

Density of vertical boundary

Heightened awareness of enclosure

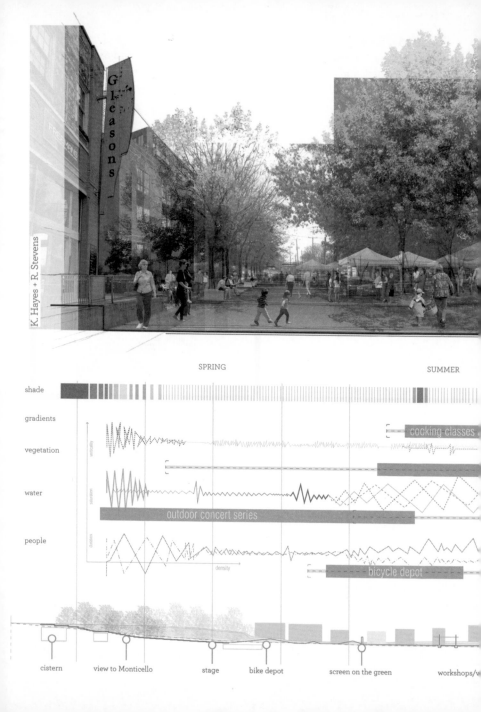

K. Hayes + R. Stevens

SPRING   SUMMER

shade

gradients

cooking classes

vegetation

water

outdoor concert series

people

bicycle depot

density

cistern   view to Monticello   stage   bike depot   screen on the green   workshops/w

"I recently heard someone remark that farmers markets are a 'Community Living Room,' and I couldn't agree more."

Charlottesville Market Central Newsletter (Fall 2009)

Seasonal program cycle at the new Charlottesville City Market.

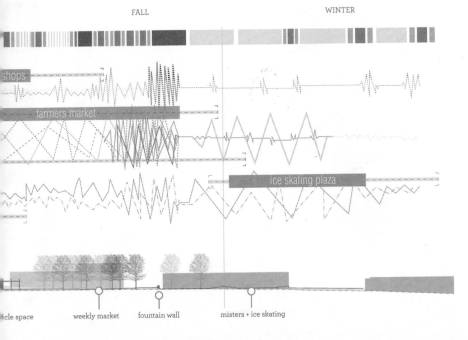

FALL   WINTER

shops

farmers market

ice skating plaza

icle space   weekly market   fountain wall   misters + ice skating

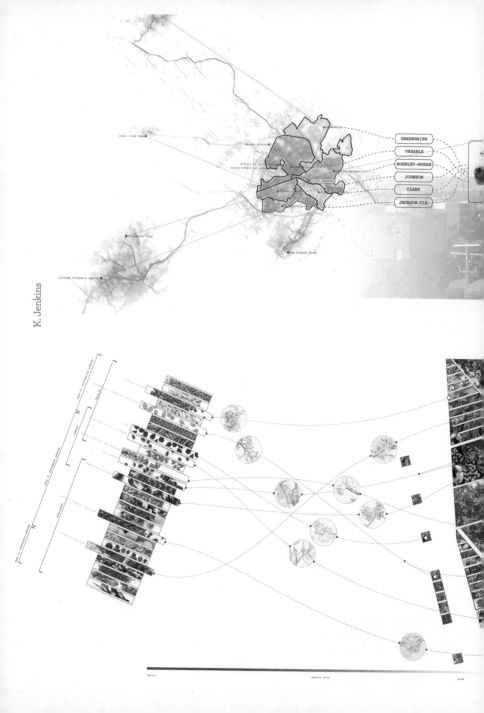

K. Jenkins

GREENBRIER
VENABLE
BURNLEY-MORAN
JOHNSON
CLARK
JACKSON-VIA

CITY MARKET

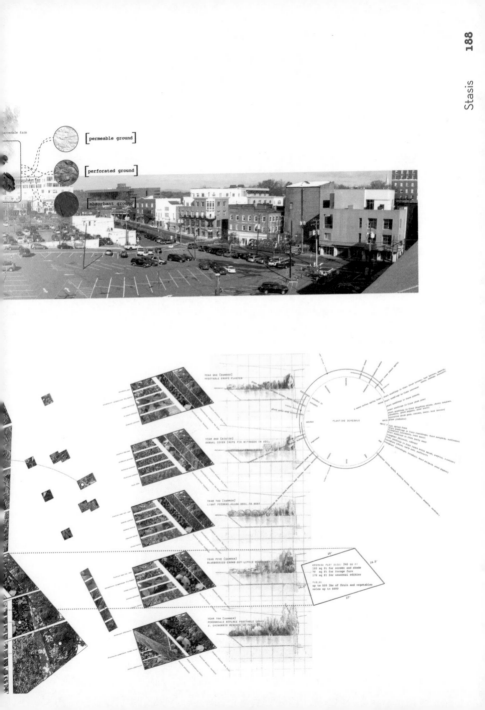

[permeable ground]

[perforated ground]

[absorbent ground]

Tout-à- l'égout

Parker Sutton, M.Arch 2013
2012 Sarah McArthur Nix Fellowship

"These underground galleries would be the organs of the metropolis and function like those of the human body without ever seeing the light of day. Pure and fresh water, along with light and heat, would circulate like the diverse fluids whose movement and replenishment sustain life itself. These liquids would work unseen and maintain public health without disrupting the smooth running of the city and without spoiling its exterior beauty."
Baron Georges Haussmann, 1854

The Hausmannization of Paris—the term given to Baron Georges Hausmann's mid-nineteenth-century reorganization of Paris under Napoleon III—was predicated on Hausmann's premodern understanding of the relationship between cities and the human body. His view was a holistic one from which he drew metaphors connecting a well-structured city to the health of its inhabitants.

Central to his vision was a reimagining of *l'égouts de Paris*, the Paris sewer system, which he describes as the city's organs. The new boulevards and arcades radiating from Paris's monuments are echoed by their subterranean counterparts, with the geometry of each sewer typology reflecting architectural and societal forces above. Indeed, the ramifications of Paris's subterranean reorganization extend beyond the mere modernization of the city's drainage and sanitation. The development of above-ground Paris—the Paris that we see—was, and is, contingent upon the infrastructure beneath it. In the words of Paris urbanist Matthew Gandy, the "urban origins lie concealed beneath the surface of the city." Through a series of drawings that cut through building, street, earth, and sewer, I attempt to reveal the complex intersection of the sewers and the built environment.

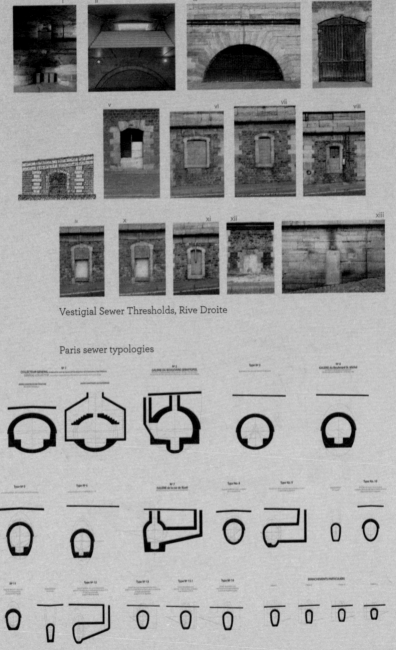

Vestigial Sewer Thresholds, Rive Droite

Paris sewer typologies

Rue Royale

Place de la Concorde

Les Tuileries

Quai des Tuileries

122'

112'

113'

Type 1

Type 7 (Collecteur Rivoli)

Type 12

Type 3

119'

Place Charles de Gaulle

Av. de Friedland

Rue du Fbg. Saint-Honoré

Notre-Dame

195'

193'

139'

106'

110'

109'

Type 12

Type 12

Type 10

Type 12

Type 13

Type 12

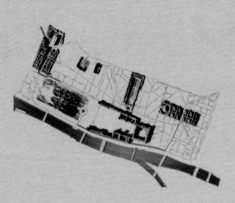

Sewer Section, Rive Droite (Monuments)
Flow Diagram, Rive Droite (Monuments)

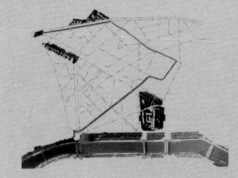

Sewer Section, Axe Historique (Boulevards)
Flow Diagram, Axe Historique (Boulevards)

Art of the Moving Creature

**Melissa Goldman (Architecture), Eric Schmidt (Art),
Steve Warner (Drama)_2012-2013_Seminar**

From giant urban mechanical puppets to wind-driven, beachcombing beasts
to animatronic state-of-the-art movie monsters, moving creatures are a
mix of joyful spectacle, precise engineering, fearless experimentation, and
resourceful fabrication techniques. An initiative of the Fabrication Facilities
of the Departments of Drama, Studio Art, and the School of Architecture, this
interdisciplinary project engaged students from all over Arts Grounds and
the University in a collaborative workshop to research, design, and construct
creatures that came to life for the Stan Winston Festival of the Moving
Creature on April 20, 2013.

Funded by an Arts in Action grant, the Jefferson Trust, UVA Parents
Committee, Studio Art Department, and the Winston Family, the Festival
showcased five gigantic moving creatures, the culminating work of two
classes: The Art of the Moving Creature I in Fall 2012 and Creature II in
Spring 2013. Creature I focused on the research, design, and engineering of
creatures through material studies, fabrication tests, and full-scale prototypes.
Creature II furthered designs for the final creatures which came to life in a

performance in the Festival
Parade. Groups from all over
Grounds participated in the
final Festival from music
composition to dance to
parkour. The Parade attacked
Arts Grounds, the Rotunda,
and Alderman Library, before
wheeling, walking, bounding,
and floating to the Festival at
Nameless Field.

The class worked in collaboration with visiting artists from

the Stan Winston School of Character Arts in Los Angeles. Founded in honor of the late Stan Winston, a UVA alum and famous Hollywood special-effects artist, SWSCA is an educational media company devoted to preserving, promoting, and teaching the art of character creation in all its forms, from practical to digital. Stan and his studio were responsible for such iconic characters as the dinosaurs in *Jurassic Park*, the creatures and characters from the *Alien*, *Predator*, and *Terminator* series, and many others.

Hollywood artists visited UVA multiple times over the course of the year and imparted invaluable knowledge and skills in hands-on creature-building workshops with the students. We are grateful for the support of Shane Mahan, Peter Clarke, Shannon Shea, Ted Haines, Billy Bryan, Johnny Ales, and the amazing Matt Winston for coming to Charlottesville and mentoring us in the crazy fantasy of creatures. Each visit culminated in a Creature Walk that brought to life the creatures one by one.

From architects to filmmakers, technical directors to engineers, arts administration to religion majors: forty students became expert creature builders over the year and engaged in a number of events for the community leading up to the final Festival. By utilizing all three Arts Grounds Shops, the class aimed to bring together students from all over the University community to build full-scale prototypes, to bring in visiting artists for hands-on experimentation, to bring together the Arts Grounds departments through the spaces and processes of making, and to foster a larger discussion about spectacle, the built environment, and creative material and building processes that engage multiple disciplines. The Creatures are coming...

Paper Matters

Iñaki Alday, Robin Dripps, Ghazal Abbasy-Asbagh
with Rebecca Cooper and Charles Sparkman

Rebecca Hora, M.Arch 2013 + Matthew Pinyan, M.Arch 2013

Much of the work produced in a school of architecture has a short lifespan: pinned up for a brief moment, critiqued, documented, and consequently packed away. This work is often viewed as a series of discrete individual projects completed by students, suspended in a specific moment in time and framed by its immediate audience. The true power of a school's work, however, lies in its identity when viewed as a whole—as a clear statement of values evidenced through a series of explorations, experiments, and research efforts. *Paper Matters* exists to pursue this agenda: to give the UVA School of Architecture a platform by which to exchange and make known the values of our faculty and students.

The Paper Matters seminar, maybe more accurately described as an initiative, represents a new agenda within the School to position our work and research beyond our own serpentine walls within a larger discourse on design. Viewed not as a class but rather as an editorial council, comprised equally of students and faculty members, *Paper Matters* is driven by a collective desire to communicate and convey the work of our School as defined by interdisciplinary pursuits in both design and research.

The value of this initiative lies in its autonomy, or rather the autonomy given to students to freely propose and pursue ideas of how best to convey the current conversations and interests of the School. In the fall of 2012, realizing that there was no current comprehensive collection of student and faculty work, the council proposed, developed, and published the first edition of *Paper Matters* as a record of the School's work at a critical moment. *Paper Matters* (the book) emerged from dialogues in Paper Matters (the seminar) and became a test of how best to collect, curate, and publish projects from across all four unique disciplines within the School. The ideas, debates, and discussions of Paper Matters subsequently fueled the development of *Catalyst*, a publication that will serve as the crucial link between students, faculty, and a larger community of designers and thinkers. The goal of these efforts is to encourage a continuous dialogue across disciplinary boundaries in order to chart and uncover current and future directions in the School.

G. Abbasy-Asbagh, R. Hora, M. Pinyan, Eds.

R. Metcalf, Ed.

C. Jennings, Ed.

R. Metcalf, w. C. Jennings, Eds.

I. Alday, A. Ayala, N. Burgess, R. Hora, Eds.

Flux

Having arrived at a point where our current ways of inhabitting the built environment are no longer sustainable, our frame of reference has shifted to address emergent social, ecological, and economic conditions. Approaches that build.on the synthesis of natural processes and built form enable a dynamic mode of operation, where bottom-up processes have replace overarching geometric schemas.

How can the logic of dynamic natural systems inform the future of cities? (Flux 209)

How can vital cycles and techniques of management and maintenance of planting inform the way we design landscapes? (Flux 225)

What is the potential of emergent processes such as degradation, recomposition, accumulation, and growth in reimagining the relationship of built form to unstable environmental conditions? (Flux 241)

What are the boundaries of growth in shrinking cities? What is the potential for deconstruction and salvaging materials to spur regenerative economies? How can the embodied energy of existing buildings be leveraged to enable more sustainable building practices? (Flux 251)

Can programmatic hybridities produce the thick, layered, liminal spaces that can respond to our changing socio-political, ecological and economic conditions? (Flux 263 & Flux 269)

On the Lessons of the Lawn

Peter Waldman in Dialogue with Citizens and Strangers

I try to reanimate youth's voracious appetite to engage the world as coincidental with life.

As a citizen and traveler I am concerned with the visceral vitality of place, with making here and now a commitment to an ethical culture. I believe the enduring truths are to be found in the routine places of everyday life.

As a teacher I serve to guide, to recover, and to reflect in the light of *other* generations' capacities to engage the frictional territories defined by the Surveyor, the Nomad, and the Lunatic. I encourage both vulnerable uncertainties as well as grounded sensibilities in building the intellectual and imaginative character of each student.

I have been exploring the space between the Pyramids and the Sphinx for some time now.

Eleven years each at Princeton, Rice, and now the University of Virginia have helped me to grow tremendously by each circumstantial reorientation. My students are my journeymen, mapmakers all, equally at ease with the spatial territories of Aeneas and Vermeer and the temporal imaginations of Eco and Cortázar. I encourage students to reconsider boundaries and conventions, but never covenants. Some consider me irreverently avant-garde; I believe I am profoundly conservative. I have been entrusted for years to advocate the Venice program as sublimely *modern* while simultaneously departing with students for Barcelona on *my way* back to Troy.

My education commenced in the shadowy mica mines of New York City, was then challenged in the prismatic *altiplano* oases of Peace Corps Peru, and has been recently radicalized at the American Academy in Rome. It took me eighteen years to cross the Hudson River on my way to Princeton, another eighteen to cross the Mississippi and the Old & Lost Rivers on my way to Texas, only to double-cross myself as I forded the New River to settle in this Old Dominion.

These spatial and temporal journeys are recounted in my teaching as Spatial Tales of Origin, the stuff of architecture. Recently it has been rumored that I am planting a new orchard in North Garden while reciting instructions from Pliny's ancient text. I am a Cabalist who celebrates the temporal and spatial simultaneities of the *School of Athens* in Old Cabell Hall. My curriculum vitae is my syllabus.

I am often asked to give context to that which I teach.
I teach the *Beginning* and the *End* of the Foundation Curriculum of this New World University: *Architecture as a Covenant with the World, Again.* Herein I teach *A Primer of Easy Pieces* with Caves and Tents serving as benchmarks for *A Syntax of Structure* while a Native American sensibility for both *Bear Claws and Eagle Feathers* keeps me honest.
On the first day of class in Architecture 101, I ask the students two questions: *Where do you come from? Where do you now find yourself?*
On the last day of class I ask graduating students to meet me at the Lawn before sunrise, to take off their socks and shoes and to walk the Lawn barefoot.

Out of darkness comes reorientation and we walk away stained for life by the literal turf of Common Ground as a lingering response to Mr. Jefferson's visceral and ethical project.

I am an Architect and Educator who is profoundly blessed and challenged *here and now* to be working *on-site* with the foundation principles of a New World Culture. Mr. Jefferson specifically identified in the Lawn the conjunction of enduring principles as still *useful knowledge* derived from *other cultures* located long, long ago and far, far away. After one decade in the foundation trenches here I find myself now beginning once again a new undergraduate course on ethics and the imagination: *On the Lessons of the Lawn.*

Biophilic Urbanism: Cities + Nature

Tim Beatley
Department of Urban and Environmental Planning

Biophilia, a concept popularized by E. O. Wilson, holds that we have an innate need for contact with nature and the natural world. We need nature in our lives to be happy, healthy, and productive; it is not optional but rather a requisite condition of urban life. Increasingly designers and planners understand the need to incorporate nature in the design of homes, offices, and other living and work spaces. Biophilic design is now a much discussed and accepted practice and goal, but until now it has largely been applied to single buildings and structures. At its core, a biophilic city is a place that is full of nature and where residents see and feel and experience this nature around them every day. In a biophilic city nature is not distant, but here, nearby. It is a city that propels its residents outside and fosters a curiosity and care about the outside world. It is a city that learns from and is modeled after nature.

About two years ago I created the Biophilic Cities Project at UVA to more systematically examine the ways in which nature can be protected, restored, celebrated, and better integrated into cities. With funding from the Summit Foundation of Washington, DC, this work has expanded and entailed developing working relationships with partner cities around the country and the world. From Singapore to Vitoria-Gasteiz in the Basque country of Spain to San Francisco and Milwaukee, the Project seeks to understand how nature finds its way into planning and design, to document innovative and best practices, and to begin to cultivate an international network of biophilic

Can cities be understood as engines for the conservation of biodiversity, and urban development and growth designed and steered in ways that positively restore and add to global biodiversity?

cities and biophilic urbanists. To these ends, the Project is organizing an international launch of the Biophilic Cities Network in October, 2013.

Dense cities can and do harbor immense amounts of nature and biodiversity and there are many steps and design solutions that can enhance and expand further the manifestations of nature in cities. Much of our work explores what a biophilic city looks and feels like, its qualities and characteristics, and the many steps and policies that will make nature a more central part of urban life. There are a variety of urban strategies for greening and renaturalizing cities, from the scale of a specific site and neighborhood, to the larger city and region. From urban ecological networks and connected systems of urban greenspace to green rooftops, green walls, and sidewalk gardens, we have sought to understand and document the emerging practice of biophilic urban design and planning and the many compelling stories of individuals and groups working hard to transform cities from grey and lifeless to green and biodiverse. The Project also seeks to identify what is needed beyond physical design and planning—what institutions and organizations, urban capabilities, and new urban codes will be needed to stimulate and in some cases mandate

biophilic cities and urban design. Already our work has uncovered wonderful stories of how cities are integrating nature into the urban fabric and connecting urbanites to the nature around them. These stories include Vitoria-Gasteiz's green ring, which circles the city and provides nature close-by to its dense, walkable neighborhoods, as well as new efforts there to imagine an "interior green ring." There is Oslo, which despite increasing urban density has maintained two-thirds of its land in protected forest.

Also exemplary are Singapore's efforts at vertical green-

Singapore has extensive park and green areas, tied together by 200 kilometers of park connectors, much of it in the form of elevated walkways and canopy walks. Photo credit: Tim Beatley

ing (for example, through financial subsidies, research and development, and planning standards that mandate vertical greening to replace green areas lost through development) and its parks connectors, a remarkable network of pathways through the city, much of it in the form of elevated structures at the level of the urban forest canopy. Restoring rivers is another important strategy, notably undertaken by cities like Oslo, Singapore, and Milwaukee; reconnecting urban neighborhoods to these waterways is a tremendous enhancement to quality of life. In San Francisco there have been efforts at creating smaller parks and green spaces out of the exiting urban fabric—for instance, by creating "parklets" from two to three on-street parking spaces, or by making it easier for neighborhoods to install sidewalk gardens. Other cities, such as Montreal, have facilitated the greening of alleys, leftover spaces that have been lovingly cared for as new neighborhood gathering spots. Still other cities have undertaken efforts to conserve and celebrate birds, bats, and other fauna, and to understand the city in terms of the many other forms of life that coinhabit these spaces with us.

It is not just the presence or absence of nature that defines a biophilic city; it also involves the ways and extent to which residents are directly engaged in nature and are knowledgeable about it and care for it. And here as well there is much innovation, from citizen science to school-based education to programs that create opportunities for urbanites to participate in activities such as camping in city parks during the summer months.

While we are already impressed with the variety of programs, projects, and planning efforts in cities around the world, there remain a number of important open questions. These include how much and what kind of nature is needed in cities and what combination of these natural experiences will deliver the greatest health and psychological benefits . What is the minimum daily requirement of nature, we sometimes provocatively ask. What urban tools, techniques, and strategies will be most effective at ensuring this nature exists in our urban future? Can cities be understood as engines for the conservation of biodiversity, and urban development and growth designed and steered in ways that positively restore and add to global biodiversity? These are new and important ways of understanding cities and assessing their functioning.

[For more information about the Biophilic Cities Project see our web page: http://biophiliccities.org/]

In a biophilic city nature is not distant, but here, nearby. It is a city that propels its residents outside and fosters a curiosity and care about the outside world. It is a city that learns from and is modeled after nature.

In Bishan Park, one of Singapore's most popular public spaces, the city has restored the Kallang River, converting it from a flood channel to a beautiful, meandering, biodiverse river. Photo credit: Tim Beatley

EWWW

Private Parts - Public Places

David Holzman, MLA 2013_Thesis
Advisors: Michael Lee and Sheila Crane

Designers, particularly landscape architects, have often been charged with making sites sanitary. Paradigms that champion sanitation combined with technological advances have undoubtedly helped generate healthier urban conditions and improved quality of life. However, this ethos has its dangers, and designers need to reexamine the assumptions that equate healthfulness with cleanliness.

Our embrace of practices that favor clarity, purity, and sterility may be deeply rooted in a visceral human response: disgust, a revulsion that is fundamentally associated with bodies (particularly human bodies), their parts, products, qualities, and life-sustaining actions. A tacit and unquestioning acceptance of disgust—rather than an assessment of its potential harm—may restrict innovation, humane design, and richer design thinking.

Space cannot be public without the presence of a public, and human bodies are inseparable from their parts, products, qualities, and life-sustaining actions. Yet bodily parts, products, qualities, and actions often trigger disgust, which compels distancing and privacy. How is this seemingly paradoxical relationship negotiated in the public realm? As landscape architects can we help manage or reveal this relationship in positive ways via design?

A more honest and engaged relationship with disgust may help designers tackle increased autoimmune disorders and severe allergies; rejection of the ideals associated with the body scale; unethical and inequitable toxicity and risk associated with global industrial ghettos; understandings of complex ecological relationships; and aesthetic tastes and relationships that may be a crucial but overlooked piece in the practice of landscape architecture gaining wider relevance, clout, and depth.

Our embrace of practices that favor clarity, purity, and sterility may be deeply rooted in a visceral human response: disgust, a revulsion that is at heart associated most with bodies (particularly human bodies), their parts, products, qualities, and life-sustaining actions.

On the Rivanna River

Teresa Gali-Izard_Spring 2013_Foundation Studio

This studio focuses on the visualization and development of the concept
of *urban metabolism* through the cycle of water in Charlottesville, in order
to discover how the logics of natural systems can inform the future of the
city. We propose to radically change the city's water supply system, by
proposing a new reservoir and seeking the expressive presence of water as a
generator of public space. Extending its use as public space and its function
as infrastructure, we aim to make the system more complex; this complexity
will be the context for discovering new languages that could inform the
construction of Charlottesville's public environment. The presence of the
Rivanna River and the physical characteristics of Charlottesville make
it the ideal place for this experiment. The water supply infrastructure in
Charlottesville is composed of a network of connected reservoirs located
outside the city. Our goal is to design a lake that could be filled with clean
water draining from the urban watershed. This condition was the occasion
to rethink the public space, to design the lake, and to think about how to
manage this complex infrastructure.

Students learned to understand the logic and the behavior of the Rivanna
River, a dynamic natural system, by imagining themselves as the river.
From this perspective, they translated the language of the river through
abstract drawings focusing on erosion, flows, debris, sedimentation, organic
transportation, or rocks. In the next phase, they designed the reservoir,

Charlottesville, Virginia
Flux
System

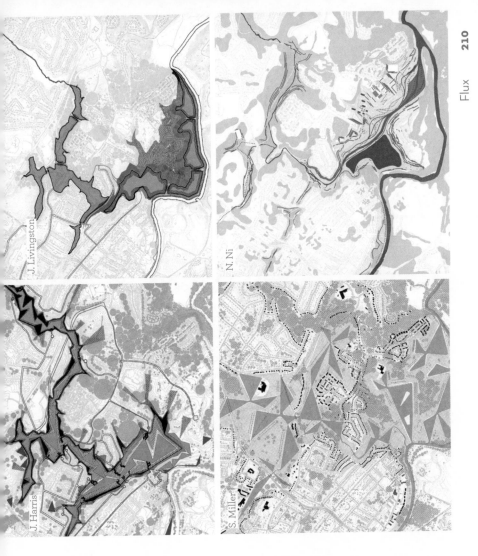

J. Livingston

N. Ni

J. Harris

S. Miller

constrained by the need to maintain the quality of the river as a system with respect to the flow and continuity of the water. They were not allowed to build a dam on the river. The reservoir had to be built on an urban tributary, through earthwork, digging and designing the topography. They were asked to calculate the water capacity in relationship to the watershed, while accounting for the temporality of the water cycle and to maintain connectivity between the city and its water infrastructure .

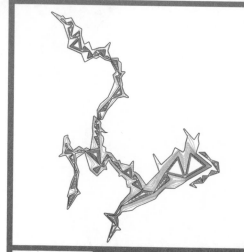

Dry Lake and Wetland

Interior Pools Filled / Wetland

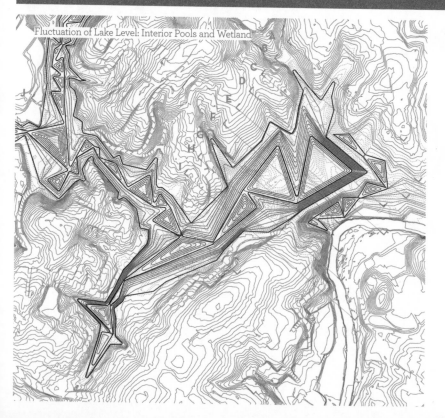

Fluctuation of Lake Level: Interior Pools and Wetland

J. Harris

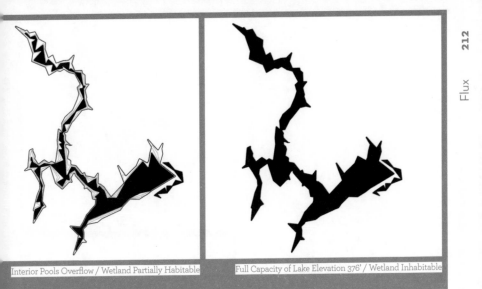

Interior Pools Overflow / Wetland Partially Habitable

Full Capacity of Lake Elevation 376' / Wetland Inhabitable

Through large-scale movement of topography, a system of stepped lakes is created that functions partly as river and partly as lake. This approach is extended beyond water to include the movement and circulation of humans, forest, and urban carpet connecting Charlottesville with this new urban/suburban reservoir.

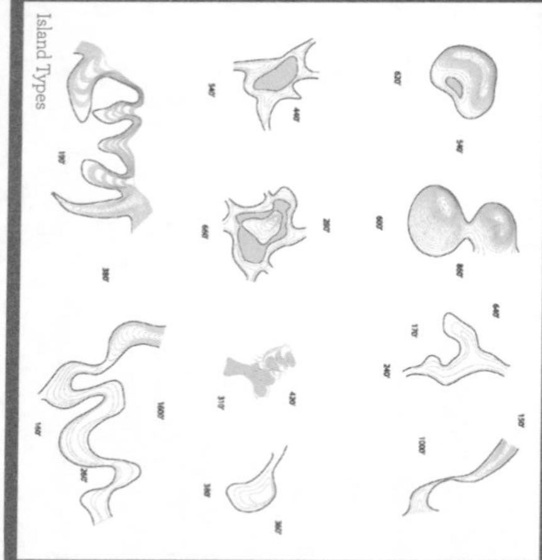

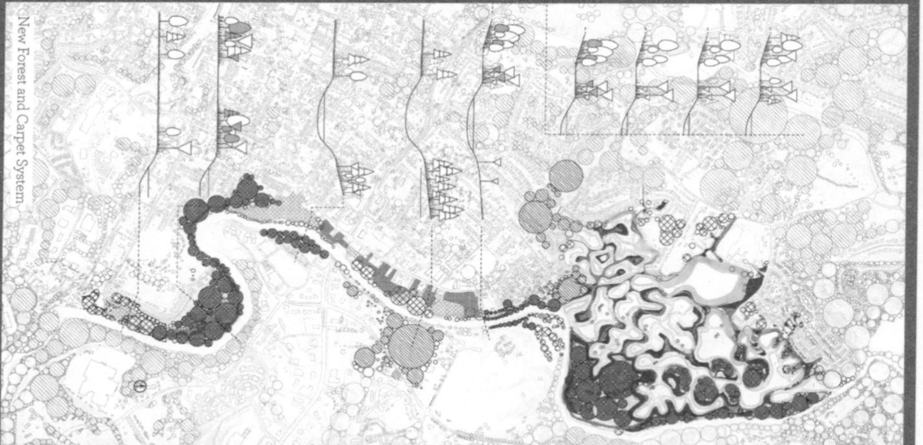

New Forest and Carpet System

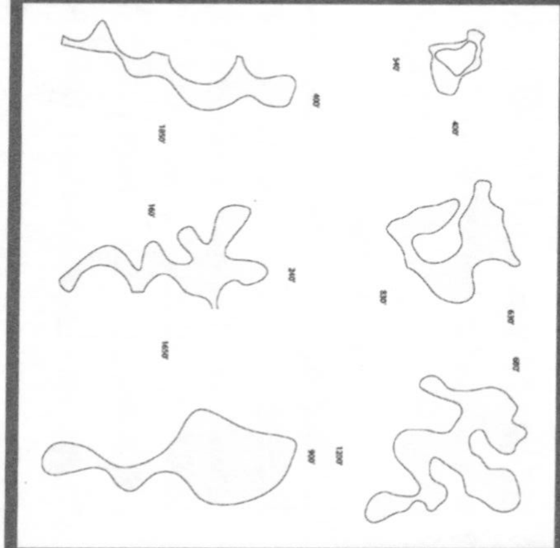

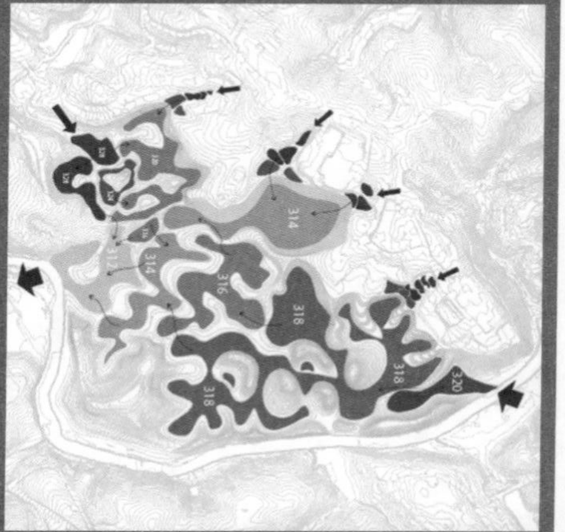

Existing River Condition

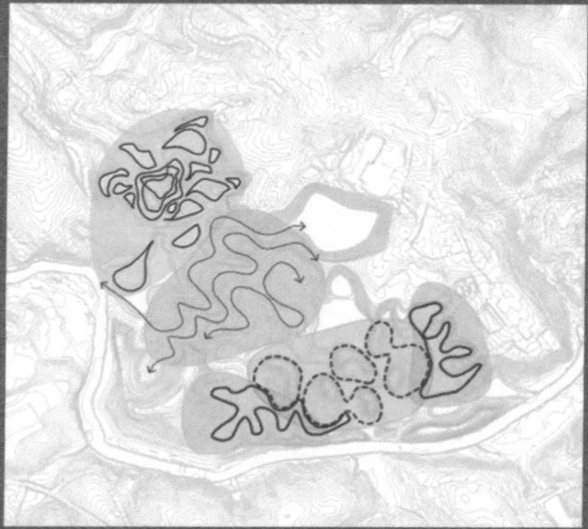

left: Three Zones of Ecosystem, far left: New Forests and Carpet system

Island Types

left: Water Types, far left: Island Types

While the formulation "water-and-land" in the design of reservoirs typically suggests water within a larger encompassing land environment, Archipelago Reservoir considers them simultaneously—as a hybrid construct. Here, the land presents an environment of nearly the same scale and equal value as the water, creating a more inclusive vision that transcends the rigid concepts of the traditional reservoir.

The Wild Anacostia

Cultivating a Thick-Edge Typology through Everyday Experience

Kate Hayes, MLA 2013_Thesis
Advisors: Leena Cho, Elizabeth Meyer

Many urban rivers today can be labeled as "thin parks," physically and spatially separated from their surrounding communities and so lacking a fuller context. This design thesis harnesses the momentum from President Obama's America Great Outdoors Initiative, as well as the narratives and issues associated with the Anacostia River in Washington, DC, to cultivate a thick-edge typology for the Anacostia. By catalyzing human appropriation and drawing on everyday activities, this thick edge acts as a guide or logic for discovering a stronger, reciprocal relationship with the urban wild. Expressed in the form of a trail, walk, and path network, the design is site specific yet is also applicable to other urban rivers and urban national parks by means of four main thickening strategies. These four strategies—based on impervious ground, tidal ground, toxic ground, and water crossing—bring renewed life to a river that has historically been misconceived and branded as "the Forgotten River," thereby enabling visitors to understand and appreciate the ever-changing dynamics and flows of this wild riverscape in the middle of the nation's capital.

Washington, DC
Flux
Type

Thicken by widening
(impervious ground)

Thicken by encompassing
(tidal ground)

Thicken by multiplying
(toxic ground)

Thicken by meandering
(water crossing)

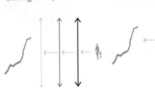

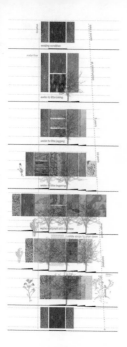

Thicken by widening (impervious ground)

Game Day: trail filters movement

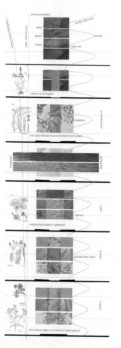

Thicken by encompassing (tidal ground)

Low Tide: monitor and experiment

Thicken by multiplying (toxic ground)

Trail marks a divide and heightens contrast between remediated and toxic ground

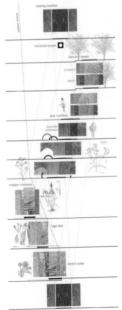

Thicken by meandering (water crossing)

m

Parasite, Interstice, Phenotype

3 Approaches to Site
Brian Osborn_Fall 2012_Foundation Studio

This studio is the first in a sequence of studios required in the Path A MLA curriculum and introduces participants to an iterative process of *thinking through making*, enabling the articulation of conceptual ideas through built form. Course exercises are designed to promote spatial literacy, critical design thinking, and a range of representational techniques including both digital and analogue workflows. This studio emphasizes the landscape as a dynamic field condition resulting from the interplay of both social and biological systems, where built form is required to negotiate an existing set of relationships and interactions. Students are introduced to tactics for site reading and interpretation as well as skills for the creation of generative representational tools enabling design strategies that are open-ended, data-driven, and expected to evolve over time. Embedded course topics include the examination of path and user sequence, transition and threshold, spatial typologies, phenotypic variation of form, temporal change, ground condition, material quality, and topographic manipulation.

Charlottesville, Virginia
Flux
System/Prototype

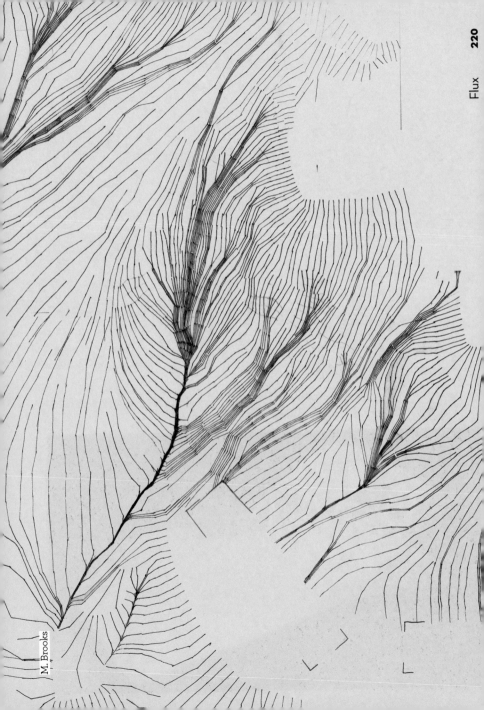

M. Brooks

S. Miller

An expandable wooden surface interacts with the ground plane to catch flowing materials and folds up to create occupiable spaces for site visitors.

Site reading is achieved with a combination of body-scale experiential observation and precise urban-scale analysis of slope, elevation, and solar radiation.

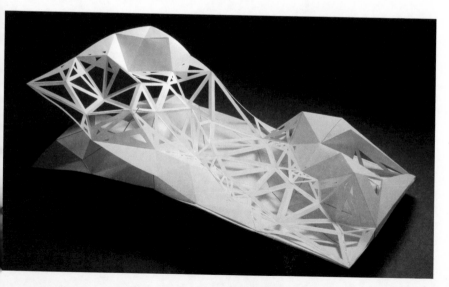

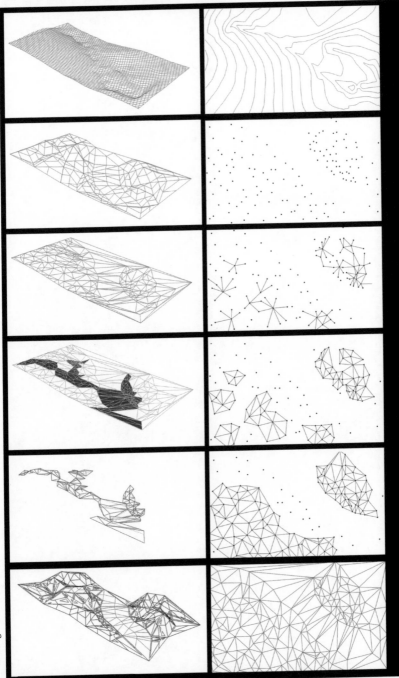

R. Rong

"In contemporary discussion the difference between natural landscape and human landscape is much less clearly defined. In parallel with this has been the development of the field of urban ecology, the investigation of the characteristics of the plant and animal communities in the urban landscape, subject to natural processes but profoundly shaped by the impact of humans and development. This has led to new design strategies that are based on an acceptance of the disturbed and hybrid nature of these landscapes and the idea that landscape design can be instrumental in working with natural processes to make new hybrid ecological systems. It is clearly not about making approximations of pristine natural environments, but rather making functioning ecologically based systems that deal with human activity and natural processes in the urban environment. Bringing all of the factors together is complex, requiring a synthesis of social, political, and economic factors, as well as issues related to urban wildlife and water management.

One of the characteristics of systems that are trying to work with natural processes is the idea of their development over time, and the formal outcomes of projects that rely on processes are difficult to predict, in a way that is often unacceptable to public agencies and other clients."

(Elizabeth Mossop, *The Landscape Urbanism Reader*, 2006)

Planted Form and Function

Teresa Gali-Izard_Spring 2013_Seminar

The knowledge of plants is a crucial part of our profession. As landscape architects, we have to be able to find multiple ways to work with plants. Learning about plants and their uses is broader than mere identification. A series of exercises related to vital cycles of plants, management, time and techniques of planting enables students to discover a new palette of opportunities to design. Eleven topics will be developed through axonometric drawings that represent the composition and distribution of plants, and the relationship between each component.

1. Perennials: Use of herbaceous plants which dry in fall and disappear in winter.
2. Annuals: Use of annual plants in an intensive or extensive way.
3. Modules: Repetition of combination of plants.
4. Management: Diversity of results using one species and different techniques of management.
5. Parametric: Combination of plants following rules of relationship.
6. Complexity: Mixing different origins and needs of plants seeking the extremes of adaptation.
7. Vertical: Composing vertical palette of plants in urban conditions.
8. Hypernature: Stressing conditions in order to have a powerful starting moment.
9. Wildlife: Reaction of abandonment in urban or rural conditions.
10. Long-term: Adding new plants in an existing vegetal structure.
11. Meadow: Meadow composition, management, and dynamics.

[siteless]
Flux
Generative Detail/System

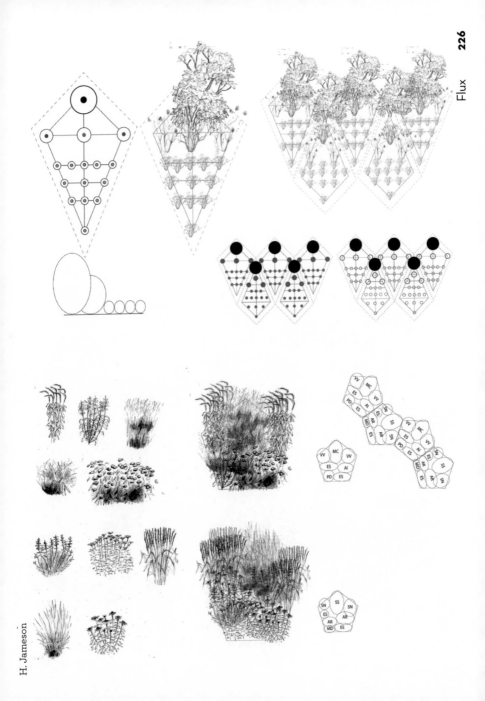

H. Jameson

Annuals Intensive

Hypernature

Module

Wild Nature

Parametric Design

Meadow

D. Alexander

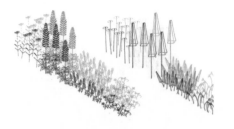

Historical

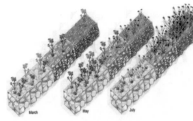

Annuals Extensive

Vertical

Long-term

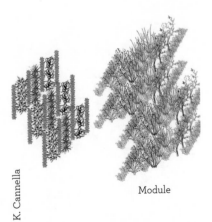

K. Cannella

Module

Meadow

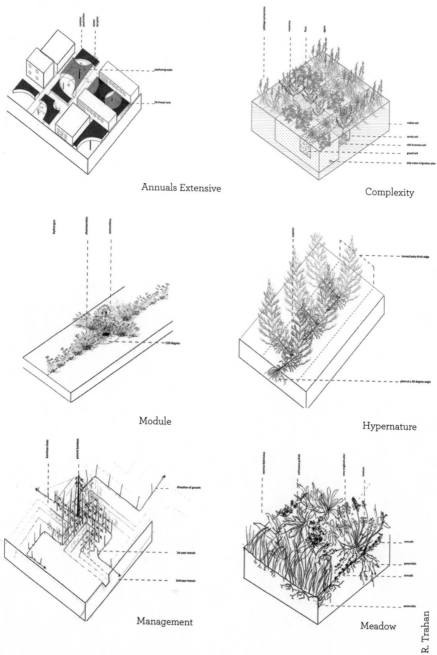

Annuals Extensive

Complexity

Module

Hypernature

Management

Meadow

R. Trahan

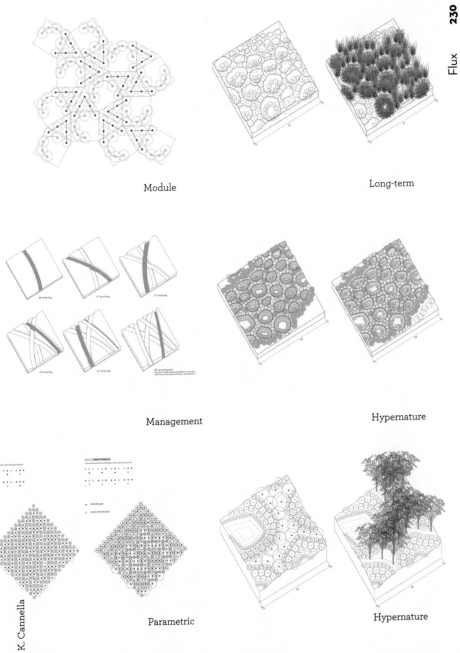

Module

Long-term

Management

Hypernature

K. Cannella

Parametric

Hypernature

Editing Emergence

Towards a Generative Maintenance Practice

Michael Geffel, MLA 2013_Thesis
Advisor: Teresa Gali-Izard

Maintenance is usually understood as mechanical operations that preserve landscape in a fixed state. Originally from Middle French, *to maintain* literally means "to hold in hand," an expression which can be interpreted in two ways: to hold a mute object in place (like a stone in your palm), or, alternatively, as an alliance between actors (like two friends walking hand in hand). In essence, maintenance enables something to continue existing, and therefore entails a constant negotiation with the ephemeral to preserve the object in a changing context. Editing Emergence investigates how maintenance mediates and generates landscape and how maintenance operations might be represented and utilized as design instruments in landscape practice. Just as the creation of a garden is not immediate, but only comes to fruition through gardening, this research proposes that landscape is equally constructed through maintenance, from the individual actions which aggregate into a vernacular, to the large-scale infrastructural services which we rely on for society to function.

Charlottesville, Virginia
Flux
System

Initially focusing solely on mowing, 1:1 physical experimentation is used to explore a design process where existing conditions generate design intent, the specific materials of the site become the maintenance palette, the formal logic and economy of tools mediate the design, and intervention is adaptive, incremental, and attentive to schedule. Drawings and photos showcase experiments in Morven Farm and Charlottesville, which attempt to model how mowing could be used as a design instrument to guide visual and physical access to a site, increase ecological diversity, and give an aesthetic signature to vague terrain. The Morven Farm component charts a rotational mowing strategy to diversify "Middle Field" spatially, ecologically, and materially while simultaneously reducing overall maintenance. The Charlottesville component uses the logic of conventional mowing paths to pattern plant succession in vacant lots, balancing the tension between care and neglect, cleanliness and biodiversity, creating "frames" to tend the urban wild.

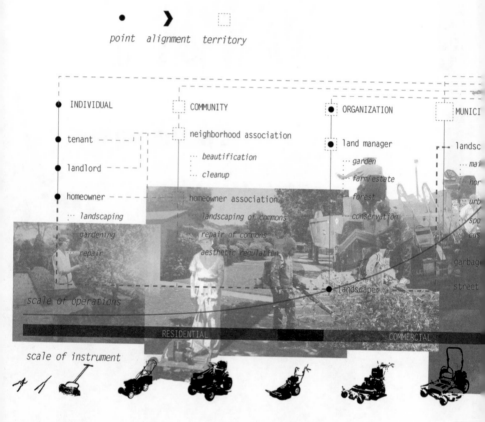

point alignment territory

INDIVIDUAL   COMMUNITY   ORGANIZATION   MUNICI

tenant   neighborhood association   land manager   landsc

landlord   *beautification*   *garden*   *mai*
                           cleanup   *farm/estate*   *hor*
homeowner   homeowner association   *forest*   *urb*
    landscaping   *landscaping of commons*   *conservation*   *spo*
    gardening   *repair of commons*   *cus*
    repair   *aesthetic regulation*   *garbag*
                                                           landscaper   street

scale of operations

RESIDENTIAL   COMMERCIAL

scale of instrument

UTILITY — — — CORPORATION — — — STATE AGENCY

sewer   rail   department of transportation

water   telecom   department of agriculture

gas   waste   department of the interior

power   shipping   department of defense

waste   resource extraction

lawn   operations & management

INFRASTRUCTURAL

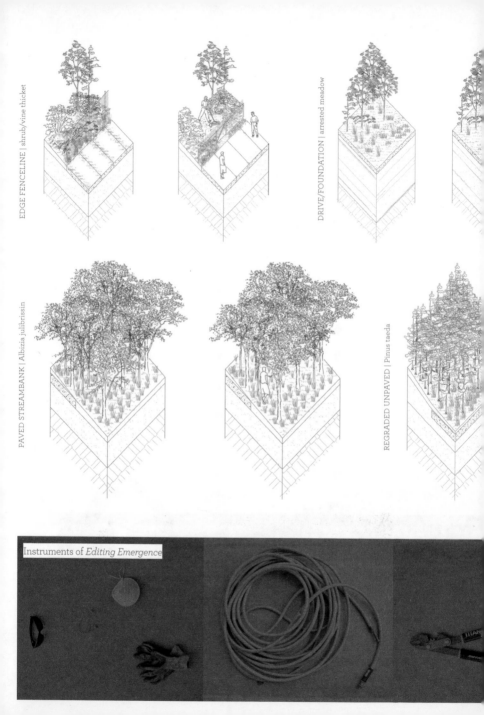

EDGE FENCELINE | shrub/vine thicket

DRIVE/FOUNDATION | arrested meadow

PAVED STREAMBANK | Albizia julibrissin

REGRADED UNPAVED | Pinus taeda

Instruments of *Editing Emergence*

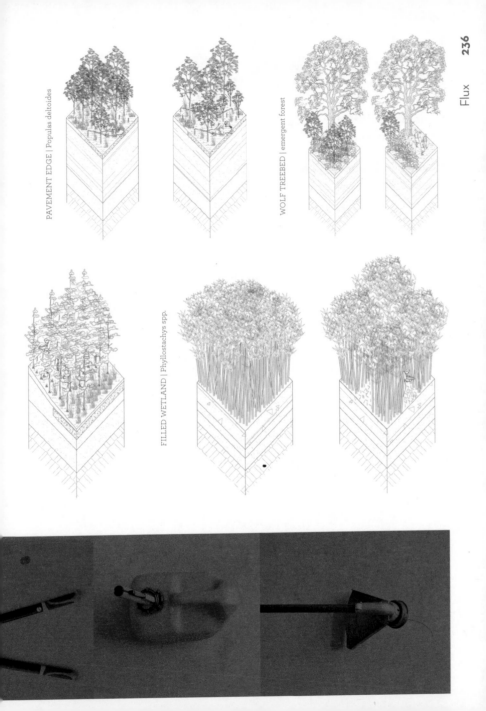

PAVEMENT EDGE | Populas deltoides

WOLF TREEBED | emergent forest

FILLED WETLAND | Phyllostachys spp.

Metadata

Explorations in the Form, Space, and Order of Digital-Image Information on the Web

Maximilian Brenner, BS.Arch 2013_Thesis
Advisor: Nana Last

Metadata is one of the many systems that constitute the World Wide Web and is an essential tool for recognizing relationships between digital-image information. The digitization of metadata homogenizes the system's elements (which include both the image and the information that describes the image), effectively transforming information into bytes. This allows for content to be uploaded, shared, transformed, etc., in unprecedented quantities. This abundance of information related to the digital image requires a reconstruction of the representation of metadata by which metadata can inform us as its own data subject. The visualizations/mappings/notations aim to critique the use of existing metadata schemas by suggesting that content is still very much shown in isolation despite its hidden connections to other content. These visualizations also aim to show how a new schema might offer a more comprehensive and insightful telling of image content on the Web.

[siteless]
Flux
System

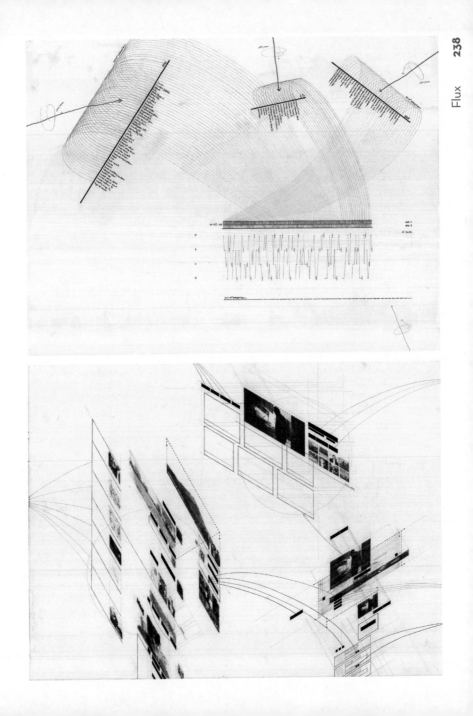

"To generalize, a field condition could be any formal or spatial matrix capable of unifying diverse elements while respecting the identity of each. Field configurations are loosely bound aggregates characterized by porosity and local interconnectivity. Overall shape and extent are highly fluid and less important than the internal relationships of parts, which determine the behavior of the field. Field conditions are bottom-up phenomena, defined not by overarching geometrical schemas but by intricate local connections. Interval, repetition, and seriality are key concepts. Form matters, but not so much the forms of things as the forms between things." (Stan Allen, "Field Conditions," 1985)

SurfaceFX

Brian Osborn_Spring 2013_Seminar

Landscape surfaces, such as paving assemblies, drainage structures, retaining walls, and erosion control systems, occupy a potentially dynamic boundary between the ground and human habitation. In this position they have the unique capacity to simultaneously influence biological processes and sensory experience. The work shown here documents a series of prototypical landscape surfaces that reflect this dual capacity for making unique places through *increased* legibility of landscape process and the coupling of social and biological agendas. Surface FX are the combined performative effect and experiential affect of these assemblies.

Choosing to consider built form relative to unstable conditions requires a recalibration of the metrics used to evaluate material performance in terms of resolution, durability, and longevity. The work included here rejects the Vitruvian virtue of *firmitas*, which has guided material practices toward firmness, durability, and strength for centuries. Instead it embraces more emergent processes such as degradation, recomposition, accumulation, and growth. This shift from the making of site assemblies that resist natural processes to the making of those that anticipate and support them inspires the development of new materials and construction methods.

[siteless]
Flux
Prototype/System

D. Alexander

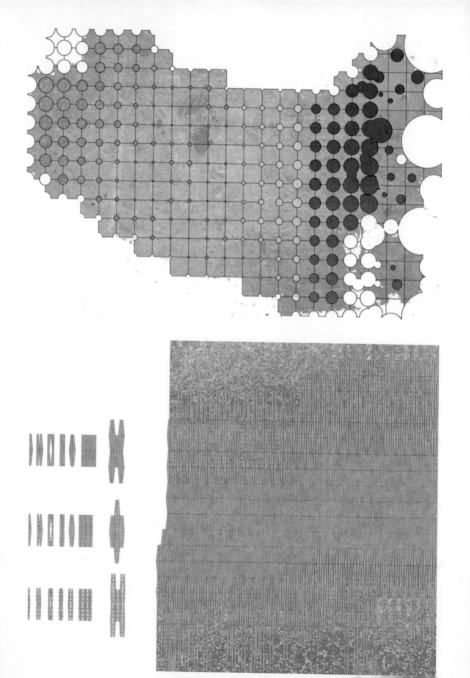

A. Bulla-Richards

W. Haynes

TECmat

Brian Osborn

Katie Jenkins and Gwen McGinn_Research Assistants

TECmat, or Temporary Erosion Control Mat, is a single articulated surface that embodies multiple soft solutions to soil stabilization including plant material, biodegradable matting, mineral soil additives, and microtopographic adjustment. Through this integrated approach to slope stabilization, TECmat is capable of stabilizing slopes, restoring natural resources, and managing storm water while simultaneously creating aesthetically satisfying forms and memorable places for human habitation.

The Chinese City

Abundance, Prudence, and Figuration

Shiqiao Li
Department of Architecture and Architectural History

For the first time in the history of human settlement, we have arrived at an urban age: the population in urban areas now equals the population of rural areas around the globe. The rapid expansion of cities in China has contributed to the advent of the urban age; during the thirty years between 1978 and 2008, the urbanization rate in China rose from 18 percent to 45 percent: 357 million farmers either moved to cities or transformed their villages into towns. The number of cities in China increased from 193 to 655. This forthcoming book outlines a theoretical framework that attempts to provide an account of the intellectual foundations of a large number of cities that, despite similar appearances, are largely unconnected with the experiences of city building rooted in those of the ancient Greek *polis*.

ABUNDANCE

The first imperative of the Chinese city concerns the ideal number of things and people in cities; in Chinese cities, there seems to be a moral and aesthetic demand for abundance and for it to be appropriately displayed. What determines the right number of things in cities? In *Timaeus*, Plato legislates a range of absolute quantities through the notion of proportion as the master key for all other quantities; the distributions of numbers, sizes, and distances are judged with strong connections to master keys like those found in mathematics, geometry, and music. While Plato regards some numbers to have higher intellectual status in the determination of quantities in cities, Shao Yong (1011-1077), one of most accomplished scholars of the *Book of Changes*, allows each number to acquire significance in its own right: "There is a thing of one thing. There is a thing of ten things. There is a thing of a hundred things. There is a thing of thousand things. There is a thing of ten-thousand things. There is a thing of a one hundred million things. There is a thing of a billion things." In his scheme of things, Shao Yong considers the human being as the "thing of a billion things," an enormously complex amalgamation; if the Western ideal of an understanding of the human being lies in the genome map as the master key, then the Chinese ideal would be grounded in an acceptance of this immense entity of ever-changing flows of quantities.

Sai Yeung Choi Street, Mongkok

This part of the book characterizes Chinese cities as amalgamations of quantities that acquire their significance in their own right; instead of being framed as having a corresponding relationship with an archetype—a utopia that holds the key to all urban quantities—Chinese cities result from quantity-control schemes that tend to accept the legitimacy of a wide range of quantities. More is more, and less is less; this foregrounds the moral and aesthetic foundations of what may be described as the city of maximum quantities, and its accompanying city of labor.

PRUDENCE

The second imperative stems from the notion of prudence and its resultant corporeal and urban forms. The Chinese way of life, morally and aesthetically codified in the teachings of Confucius from the early stages of its formation, has often been described as "sedentary." Perhaps no one embodied this idea more deeply than the Ming emperor Hongwu (reigned 1368-1398) whose vision of a contented peasant empire dedicated to the cultivation of land influenced all his imperial policies and relied heavily on strict hierarchical regulations. As Zhang Tao, a local official of the late Ming dynasty, described in detail, the ideal Ming life was one in which "every family was self-sufficient, with a house to live in, land to cultivate, hills from which to cut firewood, and gardens in which to grow vegetables." The persistent anxiety of the Chinese government was chaos (*luan*), and much of that anxiety came from the incessant assaults by the nomadic tribes on the steppe to the north and west of China, with the mounted archer as their most powerful weapon. This idealized Ming life can perhaps be seen as an epitome of Bertrand Russell's description of the prudent life rooted in the inherent demands of agriculture, complete with its emphasis on delayed gratification and the endless endur-

Urban Landscape, Zhan Wang

ance of toil. Against this picture of the safely guarded ideal life of prudence, the Greek conception of danger—as both an inevitability in life and a formative moral and aesthetic force—frames a dramatically different outlook; if the city can be seen to mediate between the body and danger, then the conception of danger gives rise to distinct mental and physical constructs in the city. This part of the book takes on the notion of the body in safety and danger by describing the resultant interior and exterior "territories" constructed in response to imaginations of danger. The body in safety can be seen to be actively engaged in the pursuit of a large range of preservation regimens, demarcating boundaries around the conserved body, the protected home, and the walled village, defining spaces of intensive and regular care, and formulating dangerous and filthy spaces of nonrecognition through the notion of *jianghu*. In the contemporary bacterially and virally challenged environment, this traditional scheme of spatial imagination is producing an intriguing layer of spaces that seem to have taken the hospital and, unwittingly, the extraordinary achievements in hospital design and management as well as the corresponding writings of Florence Nightingale on hospitals, as its archetypal space, analogous to the protected home and the walled village. As William McNeill shows in *Plagues and Peoples*, microparasites shape urban history powerfully; in Chinese cities, they also shape it distinctively.

Lan Ting Xu, Wang Xizhi

FIGURATION

The third imperative concerns the way in which the Chinese writing system—through the strategy of mapping meaning with morphemic figures instead of phonetic alphabets—works as an archetype of human thought, both as a crystallization of the past and as a prophecy for the future. The alphabet-based Western languages function effectively as systems of representations rather than images of "external reality"; in its crucial formulations of syntax and semantics, the signifier and the signified, and the linguistic inside and the realistic outside in the foundational works of Ferdinand de Saussure, Ludwig Wittgenstein, and Claude Lévi-Strauss, the study of alphabet-based language has served as an extraordinary model for immensely rich intellectual inquiries into meaning in the Western cultural context. It certainly gave rise to a "linguistic imagination of the city" such as those of Kevin Lynch, Christopher Alexander, and Bill Hillier and Julienne Hanson; a city can be understood as having a set of parallel syntactic and semantic properties that can serve as the the key to understanding.

What would be the intellectual impact of the Chinese writing system—in which the signifier and the signified can be seen as one and the same, semantic content far outweighs syntactic rules, and the inside is far more important than the outside—on mental and physical constructs? If speech is sacrificed to writing—the aesthetic constructions of the square words and the high incidents of homophones are certainly evidence for this sacrifice—then what does writing do to cities in this supremely dominant position?

To think with Pablo Picasso and Xu Bing, do the Chinese write their cities? In three chapters, this part of the book first characterizes the world of writing—against that of speech—as a world of figuration, an endless procession of figures not only as representations but, more crucially, as themselves. The figure, like truth, says Philippe Lacoue-Labarthe, has "an ontological status" of its own. This ontologically constructed "empire of figures" projects a tremendous plastic force to everything in the city; "memory without location" is one of the most intriguing results of the nature of the figure, influencing in crucial ways the use and maintenance of the built heritage in Chinese cities. The protected home, private gardens, enclosed institutions, and encircled land all become colonies of this plastic power, appearing in their figurated forms to advance the interests of the empire of figures.

Void Operations

Charlie Menefee_Fall 2012_Research Studio

Cities are physically, economically, and socially vital entities and as such are not only in constant flux but also, more often than not, die. The reasons why they thrive or die is varied and complex but are almost always brutally practical at root. The causes could be, amongst other things, changes in resources and climate, shifting political and social structures, and fluctuations in economic viability and connectivity. Planning is, if not a primary factor, certainly a secondary factor in a city's capacity to flourish or fail. Nowhere is this struggle to thrive more evident than in smaller cities and towns, especially those whose initial foundation was tentative, shortsighted, or served only a single purpose. We can all name places that were born, as it were, due to the rationale of some political entity, ready access to a resource, strategic location, concentration of a particular knowledge or skill then in demand, and/or an economically attractive population density. Towns and cities that did well initially and continued to prosper have many of these basic characteristics. They also actively adapt and constantly develop new connections to surrounding contexts from the local to the global, the physical to the economic. They are nimble and opportunistic in developing the conditions for long-term survival. Many just exist to consume until they are exhausted and then succumb. Nevertheless, some refuse to submit to the inevitable and find ways to remake themselves, but almost always at some significant cost. Sometimes this phoenix-like act works. Sometimes it does not. But the proposed changes that must be considered are often substantial. This is the problem and herein lays our work.

Danville, Virginia
Flux
System

C. Barker + J. Chang

DANVILLE, VA

The history and current status of Danville is not difficult to discover. Simply put, it is one of many mill towns across the American Southeast that has been struggling to deal with an uncertain future due to recent dramatic changes in the tobacco, furniture, and textile industries. This condition makes it a suitable ground for testing combinations of entrepreneurial and practical thinking—spatial and economic—revolving around what makes an urban condition sustainable. What makes Danville a more likely survivor than other former mill towns is that it has resources slightly above the norm. It is situated along the Dan River where the river, which flows roughly west to east, intersects with both the north-south Route 29 corridor and the railroad. Physically its original center is marked by a wealth of masonry buildings in decent repair. There are several institutions which, with company and concerted integration, could serve as a core for a sustainable Danville. This city needs to reverse its trend of expansion and growth along a 1990s-era bypass. It needs to compress itself—it needs to shrink—in order to survive. Though this is not an uncommon situation today even in some of our larger cities, these and other questions arise: What stays and what goes?

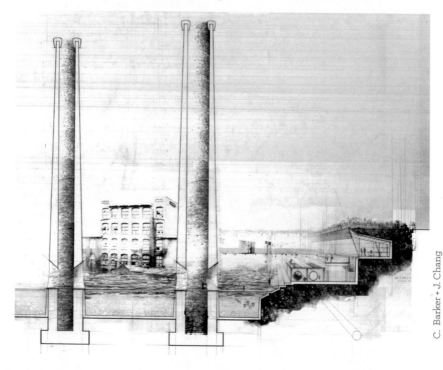

C. Barker + J. Chang

How is the value of a place or condition or situation to be measured? What are the new boundaries? What is the nature of both the place of past-and-future density and the newly created void? What is the nature of the relationship between the vital and the physically inert, the natural and the civic? What are the characteristics or qualities of a vital town or city? What challenges to the status quo need be proposed to the current community? To do a full-scale feasibility study would take more expertise and time than we have. It is possible, though, to imagine and rigorously test at the theoretical and practical levels simultaneously a range of proposals from the scale of a building to the scale of city that have at their core the objective of connecting the physical to the vital. That is what this studio intends to produce. The objectives of this studio are straightforward. One is to build collectively through the studio a body of work that might prove helpful to a community as it makes decisions about its future. The second is to strengthen the students' capacity to find, pursue, develop, and communicate an architectural argument that serves both their own interests and that of a civic entity.

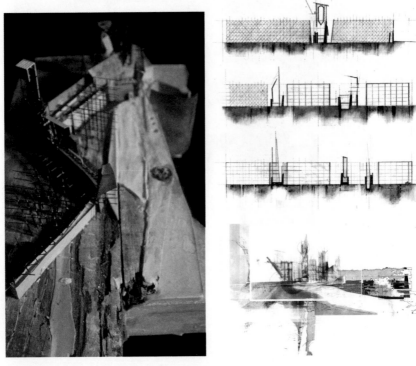

R. Hora + W. Newton

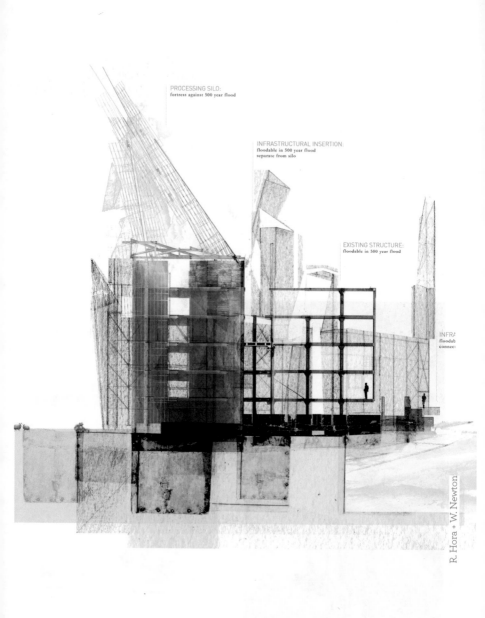

PROCESSING SILO:
fortress against 500 year flood

INFRASTRUCTURAL INSERTION:
floodable in 500 year flood
separate from silo

EXISTING STRUCTURE:
floodable in 500 year flood

INFRA
floodab
connec

R. Hora + W. Newton

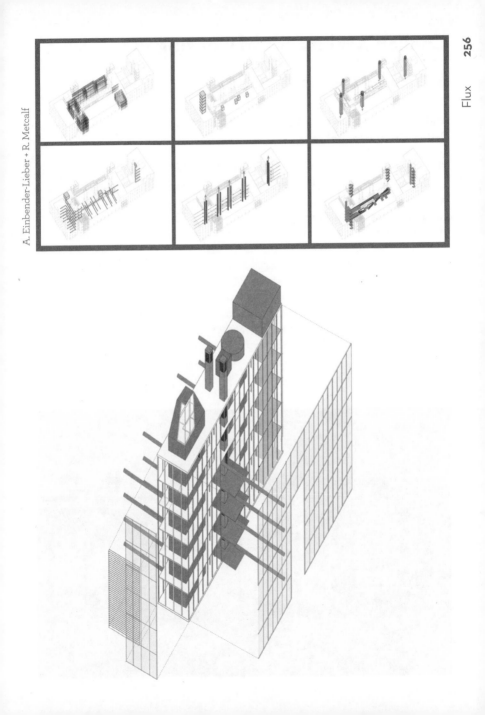

Civilian Architectural Contingency Corps
Void Operations

Andrew Brown, M.Arch 2013 + Megan Suau, M.Arch 2013
Critic: Charlie Menefee

This design proposal explores the ways in which deconstruction and material salvaging can spur regenerative economies and empower urban communities in postindustrial, post–housing boom—and bust—landscapes. Danville provides the social, economic, and spatial context in which to test the initiation of the Civilian Architectural Contingency Corps—a mobile deconstruction enterprise committed to managing the harvested resources of the built environment, educating its enlisted corps members, supporting community outreach, and providing future resources for the cities it visits. Modeled after the Civilian Conservation Corps, the CACC would begin as a pilot program in Danville—deconstructing blighted buildings, mobilizing the harvested materials to processing facilities in the city center, and managing the reintroduction of the vacated lots back into the public realm. The Corps members would be housed in mobile work camps deployed throughout the city.

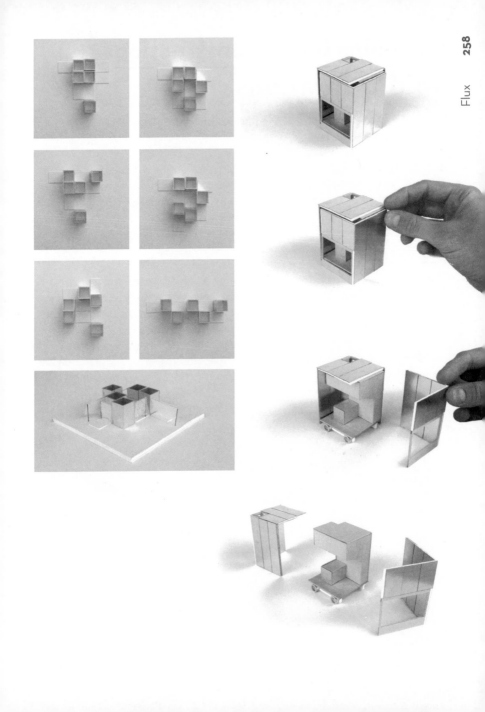

Designing for Deconstruction
Void Operations

Elizabeth Kneller, M.Arch 2013 + Parker Sutton, M.Arch 2013
Critic: Charlie Menefee

Designing for deconstruction has been practiced in the past, but it has never become a common building practice. It is difficult, if not impossible, to deconstruct every component of a modern building envelope due to the functional and material integration of building systems. We ask: How can designers leverage the embodied energy of existing buildings while designing a structure that can be disassembled and reused?

From this inquiry emerges a strategy to decouple assemblies and subassemblies that have unique functional and life-cycle expectancies into distinct kinetic elements with complementary performative properties. In pointed contrast to a conventional sealed envelope, the assemblies of this design are not entirely codependent: pieces of the assembly can be taken apart and replaced without compromising the structure. Building elements with the longest life spans and most dependencies in an assembly are constructed first and dismantled last. This makes the entire structure not only more resilient, but easier to take apart and reuse.

1.

3.

5.

2.

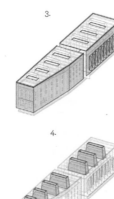

4.

1. Masonry bearing walls retained —
demolition of interior timber frame
and concrete frame

2. Insertion of screen, roof, and pods

3. Periodic maintenance of screen

4. Periodic maintenance of roof and
solar chimnies

5. Deconstruction for reuse of materials

"With building types being the elemental part of the city and the dominant types the architectural embodiment of the city's culture(s), typology as a method for architectural reasoning and experimentation for the city forms the disciplinary knowledge of architecture. Working typologically is to consider, evaluate and to project in series, by harnessing the cumulative intelligence of types. This process involves precedents, repetition, differentiation and the evolution of the type to instigate a typological change. The reinvention of architecture within typological changes involves a critical reasoning for the qualitative change and the syntactic modulation of the deep structure of type to achieve inclusive pliability that engages with the complexity of today's cities. The manner in which type utilises the diagram as an indexical tool makes it both diagnostic and prognostic. Its goal is not to search for novel forms or shapes through diagrammatic abstraction but to harness the intelligence of the deep structure of types towards new typological solutions."

(Lee & Jacoby, "For the City, From the City," 2008)

Monster

Ghazal Abbasy-Asbagh + Robin Dripps_Spring 2013_Research Studio

mon·ster [1]
    [mon-ster]
noun
1. a legendary animal combining features of animal and human form or having the forms of various animals in combination, as a centaur, griffin, or sphinx.
2. any creature so ugly or monstrous as to frighten people.
3. any animal or human grotesquely **deviating from the normal shape, behavior, or character.**
4. a person who excites horror by wickedness, cruelty, etc.
5. any animal or thing huge in size.

The idea of "deviating from the normal shape, behavior, or character", presupposes the existence of a normal condition. The premise of this studio is to explore hybrid conditions that would result in an abnormality. Building on the premise that the "normal"—the current modes of urbanism—are no longer sustainable ecologically, economically, or socially, this studio is an investigation into hybridities—cultural, phenomenal, economical, ecological, programmatic, spatial, formal, and others—as vehicles for new urbanisms. In a world where cities are shrinking, non-cities are becoming the centers of human activity, and dormitory neighborhoods have become the norm, we propose to investigate density as a possible way to generate new modes of urbanism, and further propose to challenge existing codes and practices by way of exploring new hybrid conditions. Cities are places of transaction where information, goods, cultural production, etc., all form an active network of negotiation.

[1] dictionary.com

New York City, New York
Flux
Type

A. Perez + M Cuttler

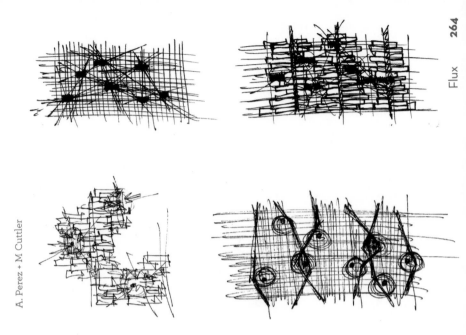

The subsequent frictions among a set of varied urban actors constitutes the pulse of a city. While the stability of enduring rituals and modes of being, accommodating as well as generating spatial structures, are important systems of reference, it is the encounter with the unknown, the other, and the foreign that catalyzes the most substantial forms of cultural advance. Density and multiplicity are crucial to its working. Cities are places of dwelling. This complex condition of public encounter and private domesticity also requires a richly variegated field of relationships. Density and connectivity are critical. The intersection between and engagement with the city of transaction and the place of dwelling is the basis for urban hybridities. These two ideas of urban relationship have different but interwoven spatial typologies. The cellular, repetitive nature of habitation must engage the fluid and open connectivity of transactional space. Boundaries between the two need to operate as rich ecotones where the greatest diversity will be found. These will of necessity become thick, layered liminal zones of cultural, social, and political action.

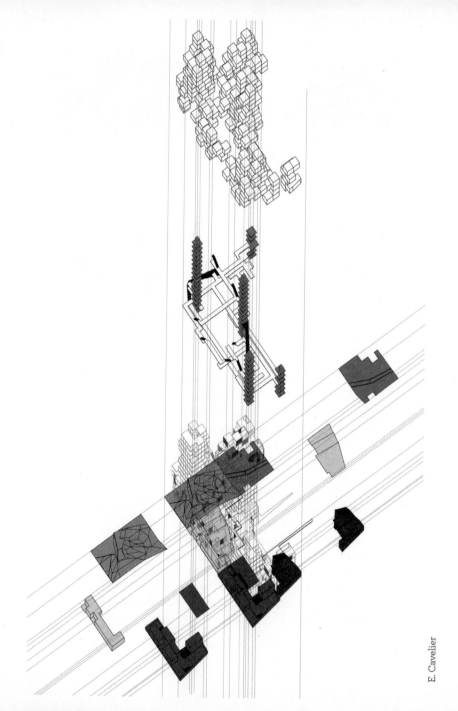

E. Cavelier

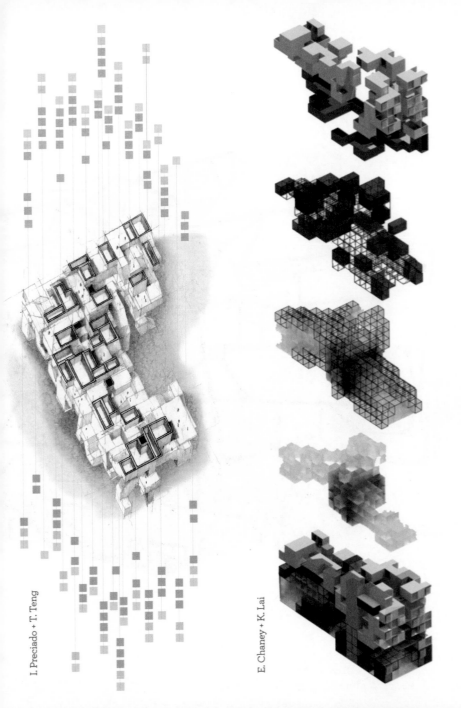

I. Preciado + T. Teng

E. Chaney + K. Lai

Flux

Philadelphia Experiments

Site, Context, and Programmatic Hybrids

Matthew Jull_Spring 2013_Foundation Studio

As the transformations of the global economy reshape infrastructural priorities and the forms life and work in the modern city, architecture is challenged to act—to create new types of living, working, and social spaces. Within this framework, this studio's central ambition is to explore the potential of the hybrid building to have a double or even triple profile and perform not simply at the scale of the building but of the city.

The site for this studio is on the eastern waterfront of Philadelphia along the Delaware River, immediately to the north of the Benjamin Franklin Bridge—an area of postindustrial buildings and vacant lots waiting for an active engagement. Fueled by the Philadelphia Planning Commission's ambition to revitalize the Delaware waterfront area via a recently developed master plan and the evolution of neighborhoods in the Old City and New Liberties areas, the site is rich with potential.

Current efforts to reestablish the Delaware waterfront are not without challenges: the search for its new identity and the role that this historic area of Philadelphia represents for the rest of the city are just two of the issues that they face. Although the site is in an urban context, its characteristics are ambivalent: immediately adjacent to the Benjamin Franklin Bridge, cut

Philadelphia, Pennsylvania
Flux
Type

S. Karpinski

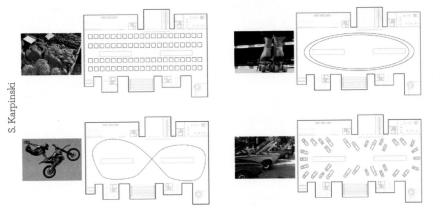

off from the city by I-95 to the west and from the river by the Christopher Columbus Boulevard, it represents an odd mixture of urbanity and pseudo-suburban/industrial park sparseness.

The proposed program is a hybrid combination of mediatheque (public) and apartments (private) that house students, artists, families, executives, professionals, and low-income residents. As a conglomerate it functions at different scales for the varied constituents at different times of the day, season, and the year.

In the interests of economy and efficiency, public and private sectors must collaborate in consolidating resources and shared usage. In order to examine the actual function of such an entity, programming analysis must look beyond the spatial configuration to the use and the schedule for the building, which contribute to the complexity of its function and identity. An institution that is both responsive to its constituents and also to the site can become a generator for the new identity of the Delaware waterfront and adjacent Old City and Northern Liberties. The program may be considered as an aggregate of two individual entities, but we will consider how some programmatic elements can be used by other programs at different times of day and how some spaces can be shared by both to increase and enhance the presence of each other. Such an approach may produce a creative interpretation of the program that defines the identity and site strategy for the building.

The scheme embraces the juxtaposition of scales between a "great hall"-style market space, down to the smaller scale of the individual apartment unit.
The hall is utilized as a market during the day, while evening brings a different set of activities to the space, e.g. roller-skating rink, car shows, dirt bike races, etc.

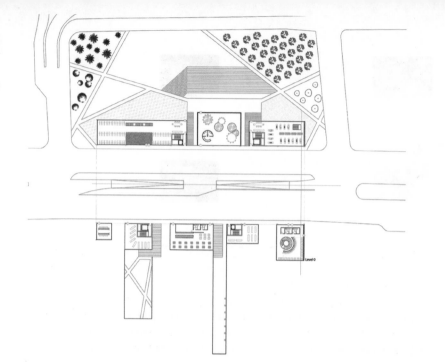

Level 0

Level 1

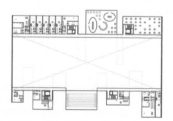

S. Karpinski

The proposal attempts to create a "nutrient network" as a centerpiece for community in Philadelphia. Located on a complex site bound by multiple thoroughfares, the building bridges a commuter road, opening the site as a much needed green oasis along the waterfront while maintaining the flow of traffic and goods into and out of the building.

Organized around the armature of a publicly accessible media center, the Philadelphia MediaTech Center brings together demand from across the region for high-tech design and innovation services.

N. Knodt

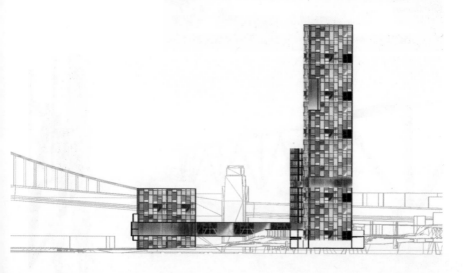

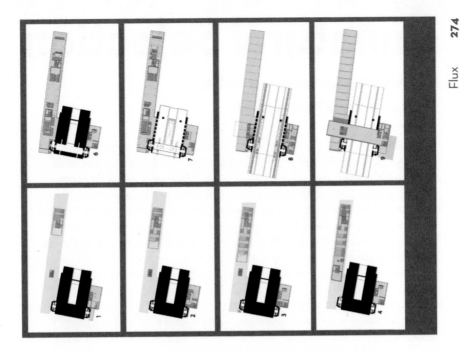

Z. Carter

The proposed building occupies the juncture between two of Philadelphia's recently established transportation hubs—the ferry terminal and the metro station. In doing so, it links Center City with the waterfront park system. The form of the building becomes a literal manifestation of the circulation down from the metro station to the ferry terminal.

Unnatural Selection

The Human Genome Project and the City

Nana Last_Fall 2012_Research Studio

A population is all the organisms that both belong to the same group or species and live in the same geographical area. Which is to say it is both a biological and a geographical concept. The Unnatural Selection studio proposes to investigate what the concept of population means at the start of the twenty-first century, a century that has been called by some the "biology century." To do this, the studio's main project is to situate a Center for the Human Genome Project (HGP) in the Wall Street area of New York City in the heart in the global financial community.

The HGP's mapping of the entire human genome was completed in the spring of 2003 coinciding with the fiftieth anniversary of Watson and Crick's discovery of the fundamental structure of DNA. At the heart of this undertaking is the understanding that genes are units of encoded information, an understanding that effectively collapses the information revolution and the life sciences into one. Building on this line of thinking, this studio proposes to investigate the underlying processes of gene sequencing and mutations as a form of Darwinian thesis in the age of mass movement of people and global competition for financial resources.

Initiated by the United States Department of Energy in 1990, the HGP has developed into an international scientific research project whose primary goal was to identify and map the human genome from both a physical and a functional standpoint. A genome is an organism's complete set of DNA. The human genome contains 20-25,000 genes and over three billion base pairs. Mapping the sequence produces a reference model, the genome sequence, which has been made available to everyone on the internet in a

New York City, New York
Flux
Type

database known as GenBank. Other goals of the HGP include enhancing computational resources and the transferring of these technologies to the private sector. This last was critical in catalyzing the multibillion dollar US biotechnology industry.

While the mapping was completed in 2003, research and analysis continues. The sequencing of DNA is only a start in the field of genomics. Data stemming from the human genome has catalyzed a new high-profile life sciences industry. Applications of the data cross boundaries from medicine and food to energy and environmental resources, environmental biotechnology and DNA fingerprinting. There are predictions that the life sciences industry may become the largest sector in the US economy. The HGP Center would be a site of continued research as well as a place to coordinate, develop, and disseminate information, and respond to the various requirements of research, commercialization, education, archiving, and negotiating competing claims ranging form the scientific to the medical to the commercial to the urban, legal, and ethical.

Many social, legal, and ethical concerns will continue to arise from the knowledge, technologies, and industries spawned by the HGP. These include access to and fairness in the use of genetic information, issues of privacy, intellectual property, commercialization, health and environmental concerns, reproductive issues, and questions of human agency. What role, for example, do genes play in issues of behavior? Or can isolated human genes be patented? Such questions lie at the center of social, economic, and legal relations.

Y. Ogunwumi

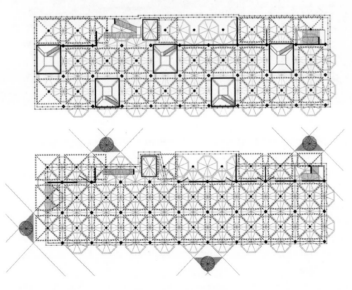

A wide range of potential relations exist between the center and its siting on Wall Street. These include but are not at all limited to the following:

1. The center can be viewed as part of the capitalist project of commercialization, exchange, and privatization.
2. The center can itself be seen as a genetic parasite/invader of the city, of Wall Street, etc.
3. The center and the site can both be seen as coexisting within the urban fabric.
4. Both center and site can be seen as two manifestations of the algorithm-driven information age.

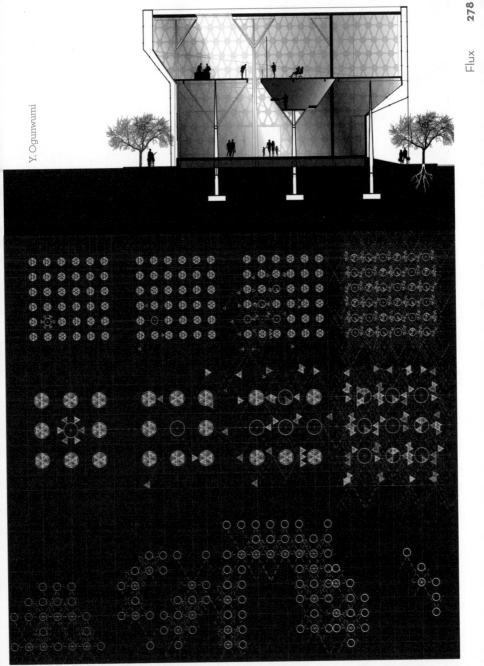

Transnational Modernisms

Sheila Crane_Spring 2013

Modernism as an aesthetic project was founded on the smooth translatability of architectural forms and technologies across national and cultural borders. Leading architects in the early decades of the twentieth century aspired to design universal, placeless solutions, which were often further fueled by imperial expansion or dreams of international unity. Nevertheless, histories of twentieth-century architecture tend to privilege the nation-state as the defining unit of analysis. At the same time, modernist architecture has frequently been seen as a singular set of forms produced by a relatively restricted group of protagonists, a move that tends to recast Europe as a site of transcendent universalism while simultaneously ignoring the movements of architects and ideas about architecture across borders of various kinds. The Transnational Modernisms seminar faces these assumptions head-on, by considering how transfers of materials, objects, architects, and architectural knowledge across national, geographical, and cultural boundaries have transformed architectural practice in the modern period. The insights of Timothy Mitchell are especially critical for our purposes, especially his insistence that we take seriously the discrepant histories and temporalities of modernity as well as the constitutive role of colonialism in these developments.

Rather than privileging roots, cultural —and by extension, architectural— analysis should take seriously the routes through which shared practices and identities have been constructed.

The seminar focuses particular attention on new critical frameworks for understanding how architecture and cities have been shaped by transnational negotiations, from lat-nineteenth-century projects of imperial expansion to the global networks of foreign experts in planning and architecture that emerged during the Cold War.

Research focused on buildings, cities, and cultural landscapes has often failed to grapple seriously with the sustained questioning of our assumptions about cultural forms, systems, and boundaries articulated in recent decades in anthropology and related fields. By debating these arguments alongside recent work by architectural historians, the seminar responds to James Clifford's call to consider more carefully "how cultural analysis constitutes its objects—societies, traditions, communities, identities—in spatial terms and through specific spatial practices of research." Rather than presuming that "culture" describes a bounded, self-contained set of practices, Clifford challenges us to understand this concept as a product of travel as much as it is a site of residence. Seen in this light, the hotel lobby or airport serves as a more apt spatial metaphor for cultural practice than the isolated village. Rather than privileging roots, cultural—and by extension, architectural—analysis should take seriously the routes through which shared practices and identities have been constructed. In fact, elements taken to be authentic expressions of a particular culture are frequently products of strategic borrowing and adaptation.

For example, in their iconic Ministry of Education and Health Building begun in Rio de Janeiro in 1936, Lucio Costa and Oscar Niemeyer incorporated Portuguese *azulejo* tiles as means of rearticulating, in a distinctly Brazilian idiom, the universalizing forms of tower block, *pilotis*, and *brise-soleil* advocated by their colleague and collaborator Le Corbusier. However, as Jean-François Bayart points out, Portuguese *azulejo* tiles drew on Arab techniques of fabrication and incorporated blue pigment utilized in China, where it had previously been adopted from Persia. Following such routes can take us to unexpected places and challenge claims to timeless authenticity. In the face of such tangled histories, the itinerary emerges as a productive analytic tool, one that acknowledges the fundamental importance of travel experience and knowledge to modern architecture. In this sense, Esra Akcan's work on modern architecture in translation between Turkey and Germany provides an especially compelling model for rethinking architecture's mobility. Akcan adopts the lens of translation, drawing on the work of literary scholars, while emphasizing the specific dynamics of translation in architecture, where the burdens of fidelity are comparatively slight given that buildings cannot be construed as mistranslations. Tracing movements of architects and architectural models in multiple directions between Germany and Turkey, Akcan reveals the profound tensions embedded in the translatability of modernist architectural forms and the radically divergent effects of transferring the garden-city model from England to Germany to Turkey. Mapping these itineraries is never an abstraction but rather a means of tracing processes of transfer and redefinition and the profound effects of displacement and relocation experienced by Turkish architects like Sedad Eldem in Europe and German architects like Bruno Taut and Grete Schütte-Lihotzky in Turkey.

While most of the case studies examined in the seminar emphasize histories of mobility, travel, and external influences, Clifford reminds us that many powerful outside influences can be experienced without even leaving home, through the imprint and influence of commodities, strangers, or communications media from radio to the internet. In a related vein, Ikem Okoye cautions that we tend to overly privilege mobility and outside influences above all else in most histories of modernity. His examination of architectural photography in southern Nigeria in the 1920s describes a situation where radical change in architectural form and its representation was articulated not simply through the adoption of new technology but through the reimagining of architectural photography in terms of a distinctly local aesthetics.

Responding to and building on the provocations of our shared readings, students in the seminar pursued individual research projects that ranged broadly in the materials they examined and the geographies they traversed. Several studies challenged the historical parameters of the course, including one that contested conventional accounts of influence in the design of the Bevis Marks Synagogue in late seventeenth- and early eighteenth-century England. Another considered shifting perceptions of Africa in the American imagination as evidenced in the changing spaces and visual culture of Busch Gardens, the popular amusement park in Tampa, Florida, which opened in 1959, was renamed Busch Gardens: The Dark Continent in 1976, and more recently rebranded as an "ecologically moral" site dedicated to wildlife preservation. Others focused on transnational encounters, including an examination of Lewis Mumford's translation of German modernism by way of his extended interaction with Walter Curt Behrendt, and an analysis of the Creole modernist forms of the Lycée Schoelcher, a leading high school

In fact, elements taken to be authentic expressions of a particular culture are frequently products of strategic borrowing and adaptation.

in Martinique, which was not only an architecturally significant site but also a generative space for postcolonial theory insofar as Aimé Césaire, Frantz Fanon, and Édouard Glissant all crossed paths there. Two projects focused on intercultural histories in China, one excavating the relational topographies of the department store and the *lilong* (alleyway row housing) in Shanghai to challenge the presumption that the city was structured by fully self-contained ethnic enclaves. A second traced how a university founded in China by a Christian missionary from the United States and whose campus was designed in the 1920s by an American architect (Yenghing University) has come to be understood as a quintessential icon of Beijing and a distinctly Chinese landscape. Other projects considered sites closer to home, including a close analysis of the narrative constructed by the selection and spatial organization of artifacts comprising the new American galleries in the Virginia Museum of Fine Arts in Richmond. By unraveling these intercultural and transnational circuitries, graduate students in Architectural History, Architecture, and the PhD Program in Art & Architectural History contributed to the ongoing project of mapping the discrepant histories of modernity.

Ackan, Esra. 2012. *Architecture in Translation: Germany, Turkey & the Modern House*. Durham: Duke University Press.

Bayart, Jean-François. 2005. *The Illusion of Cultural Identity*. Chicago: University of Chicago Press.

Clifford, James. 1997. "Traveling Cultures." In *Routes: Travel and Translation in the Late Twentieth Century*. Cambridge, Mass.: Harvard University Press.

Mitchell, Timothy. 2000. "The Stage of Modernity." In *Questions of Modernity*. Minneapolis: University of Minnesota Press.

Okoye, Ikem. 2002. "Scratching the Membrane: Photography, Sculpture and Building in Early Twentieth-Century Southeastern Nigeria." In *The Built Surface*, vol. 2, edited by Karen Koehler. Aldershot: Ashgate.

Utopic Heterotopias

India's Work in Progress

Harsh Vardhan Jain, M.Arch 2013_Thesis
Advisor: Peter Waldman

India, one of the BRIC nations, is constantly in world focus as it is projected that the country will be one of the leading world economies by 2050. In comparison to China (also a BRIC nation), the country is lagging behind by at least fifteen years in terms of economic development. This may prove to be advantageous to the country as it can carefully tread the path of progress. Currently the construction sector contributes eight percent towards India's GDP, employing 30 million people. The planning commission report for the 12th Five Year Plan suggests that the numbers employed in this sector should rise to 92 million by 2022. Of this number 56 million are unskilled and minimally educated. The manufacturing industries tied to the construction sector are primarily cottage scale with the exception of steel and cement. According to the planning commission, the manufacturing sector will also develop (mostly through foreign imports of machinery or import substitution through self developed units). This raises a critical concern regarding the future of the large unskilled population employed in the construction sector once the industry gets mechanized. The displaced and increasing population rendered unemployed may not have enough avenues to find work. This thesis projects a model to balance the methods of construction through exploring different and appropriate forms of urbanism, inherently tied to construction methodologies as well as responsive to the context thus establishing a model for development which then can satisfy the growing demands of rapid urbanization.

New Delhi, India
Flux
Paradigm Shift

The Mckinsey report projects that by 2030, the urban population in India will increase to 590 million.
This means rapid infrastructure development and unprecedented housing demand, putting tremendous pressure on the construction sector.

The site considered for exploring and demonstrating this research is a 250-acre parcel of land in the heart of the city of New Delhi. A former airport built by the British during their occupation now serves only a flying school and private helicopter landings. With an astronomical land value, the site becomes perfect to serve as a model for future development of more banal conditions at the periphery of the city.

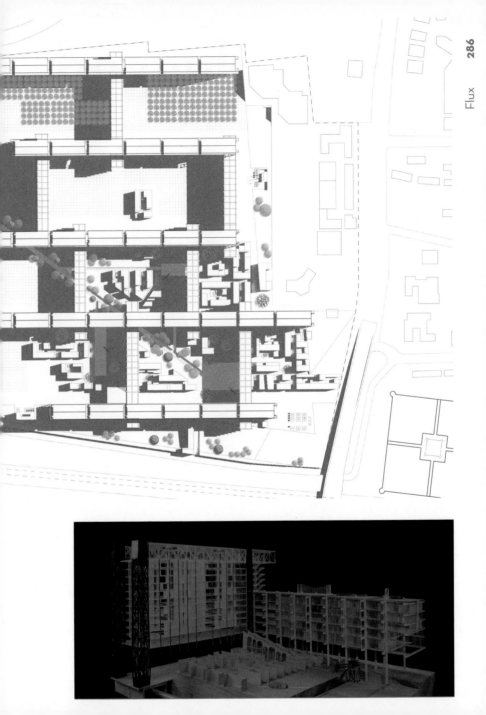

286 Flux

BIM Unplugged

Toward Resilient Built Operations in East Africa

Megan Suau, M.Arch 2013_Thesis
Advisors: Anselmo Canfora, Jeana Ripple

Architectural initiatives in developing nations have become increasingly visible within schools of architecture, nonprofit organizations, and young firms wishing to engage in design for marginalized communities. Institutional practices and organizational structures vary widely in this entrepreneurial field. Lack of documentation and congruency between projects is a result of the overwhelming, multivariable, complex nature of cross-cultural work, yet makes long-term progress difficult to gauge.

What drives built processes in regions without access to reliable materials, trained professionals, or regulatory authorities? What opportunities do these limitations present, especially for Western-based humanitarian aid organizations? Like the robust project tools used in the West, BIM Unplugged creates a virtual and physical resource which records, replicates, and improvises upon the successes and failures of the past. It is a toolkit for designers and builders working in developing contexts, creating a closed-loop system of project delivery with the ultimate goal of building capacity for both humanitarian organizations and the host nations.

East Africa Flux System

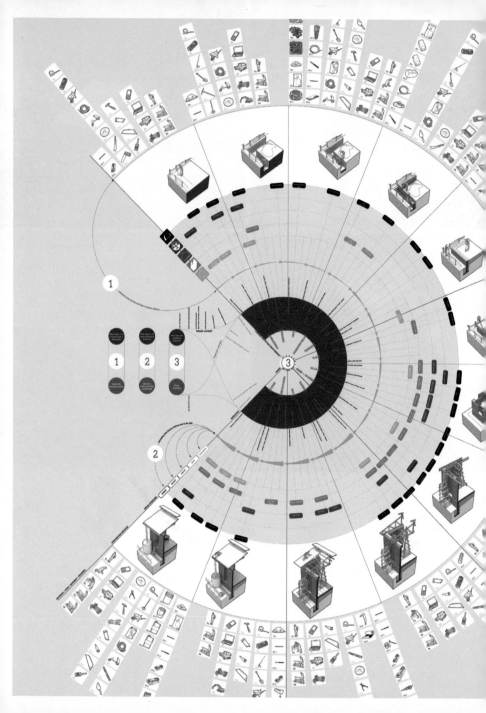

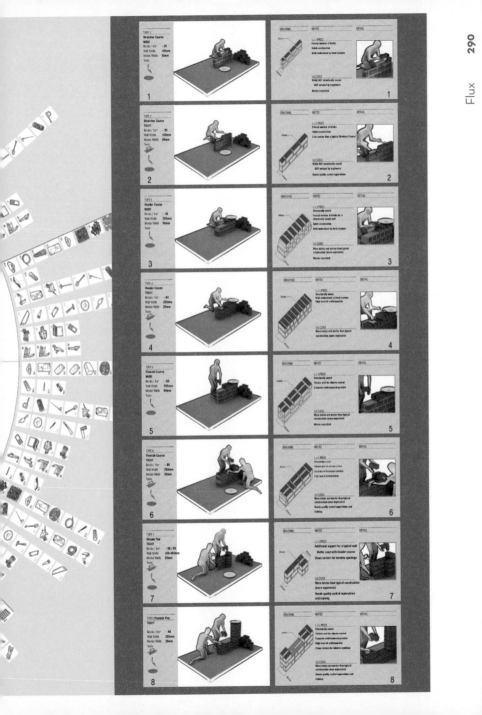

India Initiative

The Emergent Megacity and the Enduring Village

Phoebe Crisman + Peter Waldman_Summer 2012 Studio

The five-year India Initiative, conceived and directed by Phoebe Crisman and Peter Waldman, speculates about the foundations of architectural thinking in a context beyond the familiar. While applying a perspective at two scales of dwelling—the emergent megacity and the enduring village—we make connections between cultural practices that persist today and are far removed from our own. Each year focuses on one of the *panchabhuta,* or five building blocks of the universe: water, fire, earth, air, and ether. The research program is comprised of three interdependent courses that will produce an exhibit and publication of research findings and speculative projects. During the spring research seminar, students explored literary, historical, and philosophical foundations through a diverse selection of texts, films, art, architecture, and urbanism. Discussions focused on the evolving environmental, political, religious, and social discourses that inform the contemporary Indian built environment. While traveling students experienced India through sketches, drawings, collage, photographs, film, and writing. We also visited construction sites and interacted with notable Indian architects and scholars. Within the complex cultural, formal, spatial, and constructional Indian context, they designed a building in four locations: Chandigarh, Udaipur, Ahmedabad, and Pondicherry.

India
Flux
System

W. Newton

JULY 2, 2012

Fresh water is a universal human need. Individual cultures around the world have designed and built highly particular forms of water architecture and infrastructure that support the occupancy of water itself and those that use it. Often this type of architecture becomes a public place of gathering and ritual significance, where communal washing, ritual bathing, and other social activities take place. Yet the rich architectural accommodation of water has been lost in much of the world today. In the United States, for example, water is a commodity moved swiftly and invisibly through buildings and cities. Unseen, undervalued, and unappreciated, we waste and disregard this precious substance that has inspired architects for millennia. This instrumental attitude is also evident in our larger cultural understanding of place and time. Architecture, and the built environment in general, are becoming increasingly homogenous and globalized by totalizing international business practices and development models, uniform building codes, and standardized construction materials and methods. In light of these forces, how might we create contemporary architecture to support a specific occupancy, in a particular place, in a distinct time, while envisioning both the enduring and the emergent? In order to investigate these questions, the studio studied the formal, material, and cultural significance of enduring and contemporary water architecture in India, while extrapolating conjunctive design strategies linking then and there with here and now.

R. Hora

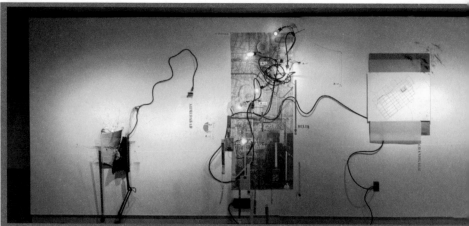

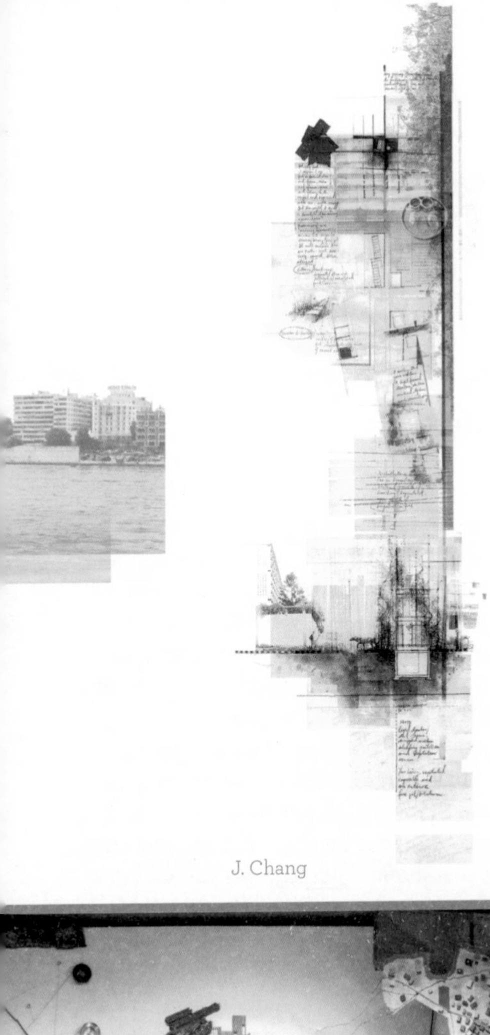

J. Chang

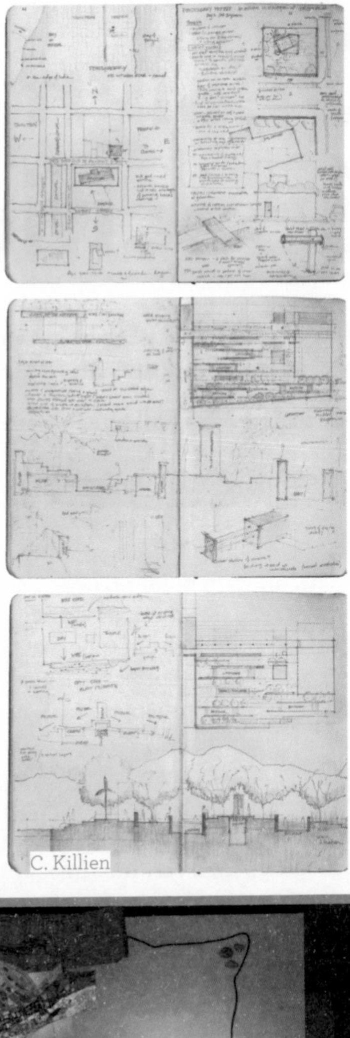

C. Killien

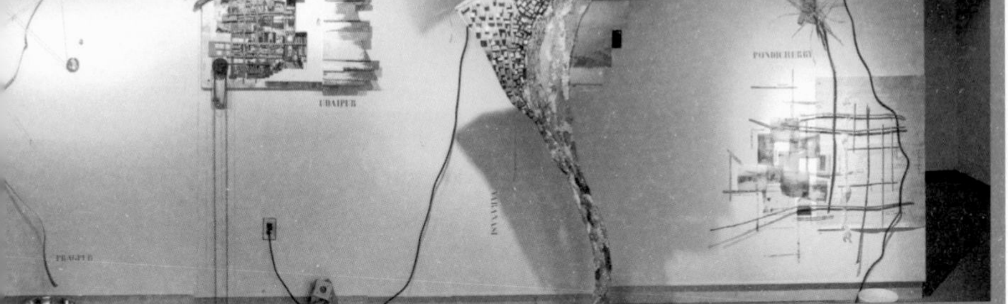

Design Specificity

Sustaining Culture + Environment:
An Institute of Indian Culture for NYC

Phoebe Crisman_Fall 2012_Research Studio

Distinct cultures have invented provocative and unique ways to build, yet architecture and the built environment in general are becoming increasingly homogenized by totalizing multinational business practices and development models, uniform building codes, standardized construction materials and methods, and international fashions replicated on flashy websites. Working within the conditions of globalization, how might we create a contemporary architecture to embody the rich cultures of a place while supporting a specific occupancy, in a particular place, in a distinct time? Architecture not only reveals clues about the values and abilities of the creators, but may also be read as a point of intersection or contact between disparate cultures. A series of design research studios will investigate the research question by working within a set of cultural conditions different than our own, so that we may challenge entrenched cultural preconceptions and test these against the realities of global development. We will also study particular buildings that embrace, resist or hybridize cross-cultural contributions in compelling ways. This studio is an essential element of the new India Initiative conceived to expand the boundaries of architectural theory and design at the University of Virginia. Students in the Fall 2012 studio designed an Institute of Indian Culture in

New York City, New York
Flux
Type

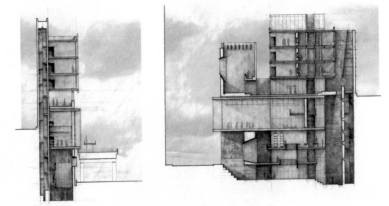

M. Pinyan

New York City that creatively synthesizes complex spatial, formal, material, cultural, and environmental issues. The Bharatiya Vidya Bhavan and Indian Council for Cultural Relations will jointly operate the Institute to preserve, encourage, and propagate the teaching and understanding of Indian art and culture and to strengthen cultural relations and mutual understanding between India and other countries. They designed a rich mix of inside and outside spaces for music, dance and drama performance, film screening, exhibition, reading, language classes, cooking, dining, dwelling for visiting artists, and other activities. The projects were designed to maximize human health and happiness while minimizing resource consumption during construction and inhabitation. The goal is to educate the user about cultural and environmental sustainability through form, space, materials, and systems. Students intervened on complex sites along the Highline to establish a significant public presence at several vertical levels to announce the Institute's important cultural and educational role.

The studio is designed to strengthen analytical and creative abilities at multiple scales through an iterative design process, to promote the study of material and tectonics, to develop critical thinking abilities, and to improve graphic, verbal, and written communication skills. Students studied the means, methods, and programmatic conditions of historic and contemporary Indian architecture within the evolving environmental, social, political, and religious discourse that informs the built environment in India. For instance, they examined how locally resourced materials and the climate-responsive strategies of shaded courts, water-harvesting forms, and stone lattices are combined with alternative energy technologies in contemporary designs.

M. Pinyan

Recognizing the importance of religious tradition and ritual to daily life in India, this cultural center is imagined as a sacred compound—a series of temples and monastic spaces intended for worship, prayer, celebration, meditation, and study. The project explores the ways in which an architect can construct ineffable, sacred space within the metropolis.

S. Karpinski

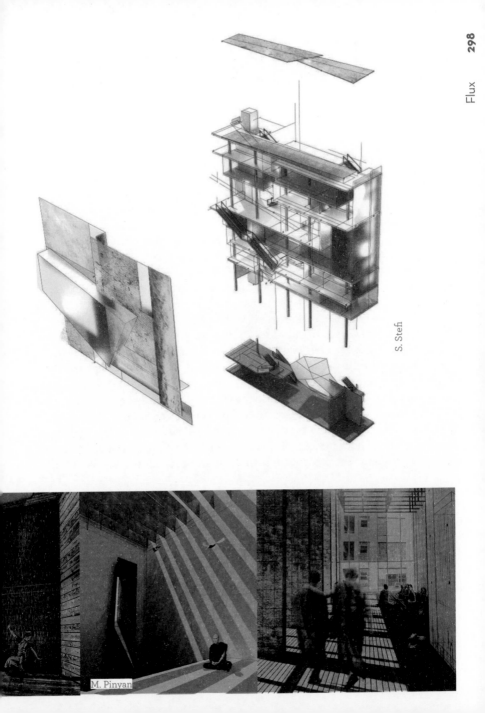

S. Stefi

M. Pinyan

un-PAINTING

An Aleatoric Composition
Sanda Iliescu

We paint and repaint walls in our houses, offices, and public halls all the time without giving the activity that much thought. In this project I sought to slow down this process and explore its aesthetic potential. In a sense the work exposes painting's dual nature—painting as utilitarian "house painting" and painting as formal composition. I might not have explored these issues, however, in relation to any wall. un-PAINTING is as much the result of abstract ideas as it is a unique response to a particular context. Designed by architect W.G. Clark as part of his East Addition to Campbell Hall, the wall that inspired this project stands at the juncture of new and old buildings. Deceptively simple, this long white wall performs complex spatial roles, both greeting visitors as they enter the building and, with remarkable ease, encouraging them to turn sideways and walk along it towards other interiors. Visible from afar behind a glass façade, the wall combines the stillness of a painting—we face it as we would a painting framed under glass—with the flowing movement we associate with the experience of music.

For a year after its completion in 2010 the wall remained empty, reflecting only the morning sunlight, the shadows of passersby, and sounds of echoing footsteps. Then, in January 2011, it was painted yellow as part of an installation displayed on the floor in front. Six months later it was time for the wall to become white again. The prospect of seeing the brilliant yellow disappear both

saddened and interested me. I liked the yellow but had also admired the earlier luminous white. I designed un-PAINTING as a way to highlight this necessary task of repainting by transforming it into a dynamic public art project.

Much like a musical score, the unpainting project would follow a script. The script would prescribe a progression of formal painterly actions that would guide the process of painting.

It is possible to conceive of painting both as an act of removal (of dirt and unwanted marks) and, conversely, an act addition (of paint layers). This project may thus be imagined as the addition of new paint layers and also as a process of uncovering a past color—white—and thus as an erasure or "un-painting." The project slows down this negative-positive painting process by adding new colors as it gradually drains the wall of its brilliant yellow and returns it to the original white through a choreographed sequence of in-between states.

From its inception, the project emphasized its dual intention: to slow down and also to emphasize, even dramatize, the wall's "un-painting," from yellow back to white. In the process the project reveals the wall's potential for musicality: for painting as a visual metaphor or painting as "music for the eyes." Rather than creating literal sounds, un-PAINTING suggests sound phenomena through relationships among shapes and colors. The "un-painting" process gives the wall a voice by creating a sense of visual rhythm through the repetition of intense complementary color contrasts (blue-cyan and yellow) of simple, bold shapes that act as abstract equivalents to musical notes.

Day 1 to 14: Timeline (digital montage by Sanda Iliescu based on photos by Chase Camuzzi)

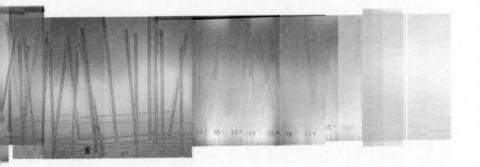

Perhaps inspired by these musings on musicality, I chose to emulate certain compositional techniques from aleatoric music. Such musical compositions are partly based on random successions of tones and sounds (in Latin, *alea* means chance or a dice game, and an *aleator* is a gambler). Aleatoric music still draws upon a musical score, though one that incorporates unpredictable or open features as well as closed or predetermined parameters. In the same way, the un-PAINTING project follows a script. Like a musical score, the predesigned script sets a progression of formal painterly actions that guide the painting process. The script includes certain open features: elements that are to be determined by chance either through the throwing of a die or by other contingencies such as the height of the painter working on a particular section of the mural.

The script for un-PAINTING includes both gradual transformations and unexpected changes—perhaps analogous to the sound of laughter or of a gust of wind breaking the steady cadence of the music. The strict repetition of blue bars is accompanied by a variable and unpredictable counterpoint. Determined by chance and unique to each painting "performance," the relative placement, orientation, and overlap of blue bars evoke a playful awareness of freedom. The height of each bar is open, to be determined by the height of the individual painting that bar. The more painters performing the mural, the more height variability there would be. Similarly, the inclination or angle of each bar is open: determined by a gaming die thrown by the painter. If the die is one or six, the bar is a perfect vertical; if the die is two or three, it inclines five degrees clockwise or counterclockwise; and if the die is four or five, it inclines ten degrees clockwise or counterclockwise.

I first imagined un-PAINTING as a gradual transition from yellow to white.

Day 14: Rose Wall & Yellow Notes (photo by Chase Camuzzi)

As I refined the project, the piece gained certain complexities. For instance, while the visual journey begins with the sharp contrast between blue bars and their increasingly light yellow ground, it ends with the softest of relationships between pale colors. Mid-way along the painting process, an unexpected hue— rose—makes its surreptitious appearance, thus adding the third primary (red) to the composition. The project thus spans the spectrum of color contrasts not only among values but also among the three primaries: yellow, blue, and red.

Day 6: Yellow Wall & Blue Notes (collage by Sanda Iliescu)

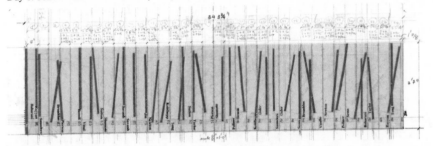

Graduate student Brianne Doak, who had experience painting wall drawings for the Sol Lewitt Foundation, taught us Lewitt's ink-wash technique, which we adapted for this project. I am deeply grateful for her patient instruction. Chase Camuzzi's sensitive photographic documentation remains an invaluable record of our process. Sameer Rayyan designed an exquisite poster and e-card for the exhibit. I am grateful as well to the following students for their contributions to the un-PAINTING project: Maria Arellano, Aneesha Baharani, Michelle Benoit, Callie Broaddus, TingTing Jin, Sarah Kohlhepp, Whitney Newton, Derin Ozler, Kelly Pierson, Adam Poliner, Samantha Saunders, Wattana Savanh, Benjamin Sessa, Lauren Shumate, Polly Smith, Parker Sutton, Lauren Taylor, Tammy Teng, and Kelsey Vitullo.

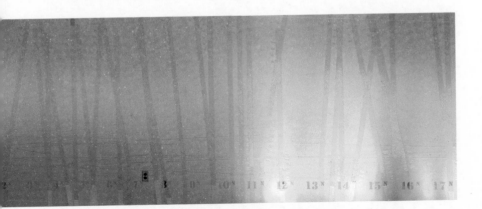

Wunderkammer

W.G. Clark
13th International Architecture Biennale, Venice 2012
curated by Tod Williams and Billie Tsien

This box doesn't contain references to architecture so much as references to the Earth. Much of the collection comprises fossils I collected in South Carolina along with Native American pottery shards. There are vials containing pebbles, more small fossils, sea glass, and soil.
A globe of the Earth is included, as are twenty calendar notebooks representing twenty years of teaching architecture. Crayons represent my love of drawing from an early age. The books largely represent ethical positions that I've admired. Bob Dylan is included because of his influence on our lives; *Highway 61 Revisited* is when everything changed, including me. Mounted images include my grandmother and places that have been very important. The digital recorder plays a continuous loop of a mockingbird song whose intrepid inventiveness never ceases to amaze me. It's poignant and always new each time you hear it.
And then there's the waving cat...

W.G. Clark

Todd Williams and Billie Tsien invited thirty-five colleagues from around the world to place objects in a a simple wood box. The chests travelled around the world to Venice, where they were exhibited as part of the 13th International Architecture Biennale, in Casa Scaffali (House of Shelves), in the northeast garden of the Arsenale site, chosen by the curators as a "wunderkammer."

"As architects and artists we draw inspirations from the most unlikely everyday objects. These things often provide a clue as to how we think, what moves our work. We have been acquiring objects from around the world for many years. These objects have become, in a sense, a part of the DNA of their work as designers"
(Tod Williams, Billie Tsien)

lunch

Design Journal of UVA School of Architecture

And would it have been worth it, after all,
After the cups, the marmalade, the tea,
Among the porcelain, among some talk of you and
me,
Would it have been worth while,
To have bitten off the matter with a smile, ...
-T.S. Eliot

The term "lunch" is an informal derivation of the word "luncheon." Originally selected to describe the student-run design journal, the colloquialism
coupled with some "talk of you and me" speaks to the core intention of this
collection. *lunch* is inspired by chance: by chance discussions that grow
from a meal in a shared setting and by chance discussions that alter or challenge views of the space and place we inhabit. *lunch* provides for the meeting of diverse voices in a common place tended by a casual atmosphere.
"To lunch" suggests an escape from the day's work, perhaps even a break.

Lunch is published with initial support from the Council for the Arts and the School of
Architecture Foundation at the University of Virginia.

Assistant editors
Sarah Brummett, Sarah Beth
McKay, Tammy Teng
Advising Editors
Jack Cochran, Nathan Burgess
Team
Enrique Cavalier, Alan Ford,
Paul Golisz, Carolina Gutierrez,
Jared Huggins, Lain Jiang,
Peter Kempson, Julia Kwolyk,
Heather Medlin,
Margaret Nersten, Polly Smith,
Rachelle Trahan

Lunch 8: Futures for Sites Unknown

Lunch 8 tackles the uncharted waters and unsteady ground facing designers.
Boundaries are being redrawn due to rising sea levels.
The large modern infrastructural projects of the mid-twentieth century are
now our antiquity and new technologies respond to craft, climate, and waste.
Ever-expanding and decentralizing patterns of urbanization are providing
vacancies and urban wilds ripe for investment. Site is not only geographic,
but a concatenation of the social, cultural, economic, ecological, and
metaphysical. It is at once bounded and boundless. It is territory, which is
implicitly contested—it is a claimed sphere of influence and therefore defines
a sphere of action. This is an incredibly exciting time to be a designer. In
this moment of uncertainty, we must ask ourselves: How do we address the
problems on the horizon when we are only starting to have a glimpse of what
they will be?

Editors: Danielle Alexander, Nicholas Knodt, Clayton Williams

snack

A *lunch* Publication

snack, the newest initiative of the *lunch* journal, is a short-run publication printed frequently throughout the year to feature the work of practitioners and lecturers that visit the School of Architecture. *snack* is currently funded by the Council for the Arts at the University of Virginia.

Editors
Danielle Alexander, Jack Cochran, Nicholas Knodt, Clayton Williams

Kate Orff (SCAPE, New York) in conversation with Heather Medlin (M.Arch '14), Danielle Alexander (MLA '14): James Moore (MLA '13), Jack Cochran (M.Arch + MUEP '13)

Heather Medlin How did you conceive of *Petrochemical America* as a project?
Kate Orff I was going to talk about one landscape that was a window into the issues of that region; in this case, it was about the United States. I asked, "What has happened in the American landscape in the last one hundred years and how profoundly has it changed?" I began trying to actually think back to one person's life and how things have changed in one hundred years. In my grandmother's town in Iowa, for example, her family was the first family in that whole area to have a car. I decided to do a snapshot of what's happened in one hundred years in these regions and pick a case study to show the change.
Danielle Alexander How did your collaboration with Robert Misrach guide the project?
Kate Orff When Richard was photographing the region in '98, he snuck into a lot of places under the cover of fog and night. I used these images to draw what I call "through lines." Each chapter is a through line, which is a thesis that links several different photographs through drawing and narrative text. As I started to work on the book it became very clear that I was looking at the small regional history and the very local and very significant dynamics between small communities and these big industrial plants that are right next door. But then you very quickly scale out to a huge regional issue. This is about American consumption patterns, our dependence on oil, and proliferation of petrochemicals in every thing from medicine to cups to pens to houses to building materials.

"The fact is that the waste lives in the landscape, is stored in the landscape, and is part of a new waste ecology. But the waste lives in all of us as well." Kate Orff

Adam Yarinsky (ARO, New York) in conversation with Jack Cochran (M.Arch + MUEP '13), Grey Elam (MLA '14), Nick Knodt (M.Arch '14), Alan Ford (M.Arch '14)

Jack Cochran It is obviously very fitting that you are here right after Tropical Storm Sandy. We were hoping to talk about the effects of that on your practice. I understand that your were part of a team with dlandstudio that produced the project New Urban Ground for the critical show Rising Currents at MoMA. How did you become involved in this project? Or rather, how did you become interested in this issue?

Adam Yarinsky Our involvement with the issues of rising sea levels started, actually, with a competition that we won in the fall of 2006 that was sponsored by the History Channel—it was called "The City of the Future." We won the New York leg of that; there were nine or ten teams that were invited to do a one-week charrette where you could envision anything you wanted, but it was to be about Manhattan specifically, one hundred years in the future. So, we chose—we were the only team that chose this—to look at the impact of rising sea levels on the developed portions of Manhattan. Our design proposition was a series of horizontal skyscrapers—pier-like buildings—that we thought of as a way of building within the road right-of-way in a flooded area. It's a kind of reinforced concrete infrastructure that could then be fit out with a variety of uses over time but be a kind of public investment in this infrastructure that would be elevated above the flooded area. It would then perpetuate inhabitation or occupation of the water's edge. At the time of that competition, we based our study on two things, really. We looked at Egbert Viele's Water Map of Manhattan from 1865; it shows the wetlands and low-lying areas of Manhattan which, even back then, were in many cases covered over or eradicated by development or landfill. We paired that with, on a conceptual level, the street grid and how that became this kind of matrix that promoted development. We thought of it as this kind of carpet-like grid, essentially, that just covered the land all the way to the tip of Manhattan.

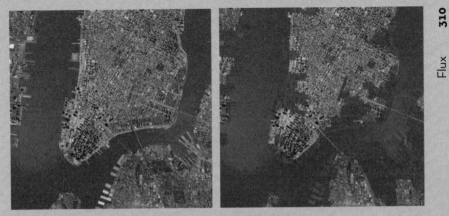

"We paired those two things [the 1865 Map of Manhattan's wetlands and low-lying areas and the street grid] and thought about the physical street as a kind of solid rather than a void that would then be built out." Adam Yarinsky

Jefferson's Legacy, NOW.

Robin Dripps [RD] and Karen Van Lengen [KVL] in conversation with the *Catalyst* editors: Ghazal Abbasy-Asbagh [GAA], Rebecca Hora [RH], Ryan Metcalf [RM], and Matthew Pinyan [MP]

RD *The Charlottesville Tapes* was a way to bring some attention to a school that had been doing excellent work that had yet to be recognized in the larger architectural community. Jacque Robertson had the idea to see what would happen if you took a group of the most well-known architects and put them in a room for a weekend without any audience and have them talk candidly about things of importance. The intellectual background was the rising influence of postmodernism and how these architects were responding. The talk was alarmingly frank, often personal, and not a little strange at times.

GAA We should bring some of this back?!

RD William Williams, who was teaching here in what would've been the twenty-fifth anniversary of that event, wanted to do just that. The interesting as well as problematic part came when trying to come up with names. For the first event it was easy. With some exceptions and probably a few contentious choices these were the icons of architecture. But twenty-five years later the hierarchy had flattened considerably, the disciplinary boundaries were rapidly expanding, and the location of important work was no longer concentrated in a few places. William's list was interesting. There were many people I hardly knew, and a number of possible candidates were not even architects in the limited sense of the term. The first event had such iconic figures that debate amongst them should have been on a near-heroic level. Of course, it wasn't. Whereas the revisit of the idea would have been more a discussion of many emergent modes of action among a group of people less certain about their direction and less eager to defend it. It therefore would have been a bit more productive.

GAA For me a great incentive in working on this book was to understand what is going on here. When I arrived here last August the sense that I got was that everyone here is really invested in the environment, be it the political and social environment, or the climatic conditions. Consequently, I think that to a certain extent we're less immersed in certain disciplinary discourse, and perhaps this is now the discourse of the moment, and it may very well be that we are really facing a paradigm shift in disciplinary terms. What I often wonder is, if we were to recreate the *Charlottesville Tapes* who would you invite?

Will we be inviting architects? Or would they be from other disciplines, doing other things that we may find relevant, or we could learn from, as was the case with the two symposia that took place here in the spring semester.

RD I think that will be the case. The discipline was more easily grasped then. Even the more obvious inputs of structural engineering, environmental control, and perhaps systems of construction were rarely acknowledged in the discourse other than as enablers of an a priori architectural idea. So assembling this rather small group of architects made sense as a window into what was going on at the time. But that certainly has changed. If you were to metaphorically lift the hood of a recent architectural project, you are likely to find some of the major influences coming from structural engineers, environmental planners, material researchers, fabricators, computer scientists, and an expanding list of researchers working in areas not even imagined all that long ago. Then there are the video game designers and computer animators that are equally crucial contributors. This is the current discipline of architecture. This expanded field raises many unsettling questions about who we really are and what is it that makes us unique. Equally disturbing is confronting what exactly we need to know. Look what is going on here. We get a new CNC capability on a yearly basis and this requires mechanical and electronic skills

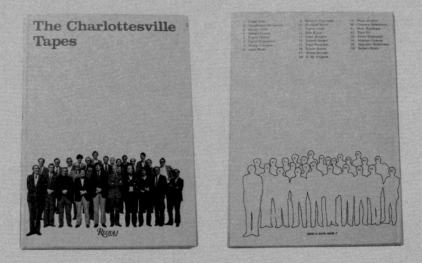

The Charlottesville Tapes: Transcript of Conference at the University of Virginia School of Architecture Charlottesville, Virginia November 12 and 13 1982 (Rizzoli, 1985)

along with code writing, program hacking, and other new areas of knowledge. Recent structural and environmental simulation software allow architects to take on areas that used to be the exclusive domain of others. Fabricating, casting, and even sewing are regular activities in the school. A curriculum can get filled very rapidly without mention of architecture. It does, however, leave unanswered, the question what is unique to the discipline, what is the core, or, perhaps, is there a core?

I have been bemused over the years at hearing the terms "formal" or "formalism" used as an epithet. Architects make things and things inevitably have form so it seems reasonable that we would be interested in form and willing to admit it. And if form is important then we should be developing a rigorous set of practices, modes of thinking, and terminology in order to discuss, create, manipulate, and represent the outcomes of critical formal operations.

I would like to think that our students are constantly interrogating forms of all sorts by taking them apart, making hypotheses about how they were held together, and then turning this around to imagine inventive ways of putting it all back together. The problem with an open embrace of form comes in part from working in a context where the weather is changing, seas are rising, economic distribution is miserable, making a concern with form seem a distraction from real problems. Form seems static, perhaps little removed from those Platonic solids that no longer hold attention. Architects are creative so how could yet another cube be anything but an admission of inventive exhaustion.

KVL Robin makes excellent points. I would like to pull apart the question of our School's personality from the larger question of the role of architecture in our culture. To the latter concern, I have always understood our professional role as akin to a symphony conductor. One needs to understand the potential of all of the players in order to create the process for a collaborative performance that is greater than any one single part. And as Robin has pointed out

that territory is much larger than it used to be so our challenges are different than fifty years ago. I do believe that form matters; however, the process of form making is today a more complex one, with a larger emphasis on process, that inevitably leads us into new territories and new formal relationships. As architects we are challenged to understand many vocab-

"The relationships [of the Lawn] are not always ideal and as such create the condition for negotiation and sharing of diverse perspectives and actions. In a way its deepest character comes from its imperfection." Karen Van Lengen

ularies, processes, and potential contributions of diverse players. Our art lies in creatively bringing them together in a formal set of relationships. This requires a wide and diverse set of experiences and a great deal of humility . In the many years I have been in Virginia, I have witnessed our School progressively take on these larger territories of investigation, e.g., landscape architecture, climatic changes, cultural diversities, material performance and technological innovation, etc. Our location in a nonurban environment has been supportive of these investigations, where faculty are willing to explore the unknown and new conditions with a focus that comes from being outside of an urban context—sometimes at the risk of formal incompletion. I think if your education teaches you anything, it has to teach you how to ask the right questions and then how to pull those answers together into a formal and coherent whole. It is important to know what you know and equally important to know what you don't know and how to find out. Developing a personal and conversant process is deeply important in today's world and is at the core of a good educational process. I believe we all struggle with that, as students, as teachers, and as professionals.

MP We talk a lot about the "what" of architecture but I'm wondering what you think about the "why" of our School. Why do we do what we do and what are the things that drive these experiments? You talked about this idea that because we are sort of divorced from the world we have set up this whole laboratory. If you had to say what you think are the driving forces...

KVL We cannot and should not escape from our own cultural underpinnings. The Academical Village is deeply important to the logic of this institution. I had the unique opportunity to live on the Lawn for eleven years during my deanship. I have understood this piece of architecture, landscape architecture, and planning to represent the aspiring values of an emerging democracy. For me, the most convincing aspects of the Lawn are the built relationships between the various parts that serve to create opportunities for interaction at many levels. Its formal aspects are experimental and in so many ways unresolved, with awkward intersections with some messy situations with formal perfection having given into process and experimentation. I think we like it for that reason. The architecture is in the service of the unpredictable and is always in constant evolution, and yet there is the sense of the whole—that we, as individuals do live in a collective world together operating separately and in relation to one another and the landscape beyond. These relationships are not always ideal and as such create the condition for negotiation and sharing of diverse perspectives and actions. In a way its deepest character comes from its imperfection. We're not on the Lawn everyday, but it's on our back. To me, the aura of this School begins there.

RD The important thing for me is that the Lawn is based on a very simple but very effective diagram that's been around forever. Therefore, when you say the Lawn is not perfect, you're measuring its physical reality against the many versions of architecture that have been based on that diagram. Most of these examples adhered strictly to the diagrammatic directives and therefore were highly resolved projects. That resolution comes with a price. Jefferson's details would fail the test of coherency required of academic architecture. But this is not the result of an uneducated architect, but rather of a powerful intellect aware of a more complex and inclusive world. For instance, many details that are considered awkward arise because Jefferson understood and valued the land. Rather than denying its existence, his architecture came undone at critical junctures in response to local topographic particularity. Architecture for Jefferson was much larger than mere building and his details are a wonderful revelation of the nuances of this thinking.

KVL Yes, here we understand architecture as both idea and process as well as product.

RD The other thing that I think is important about this place, something that I learned from Jacque Robertson, when he talked about the provincial nature of the school, not as a derogatory comment, but as a positive point.

"Our location has been supportive of these investigations, where faculty are willing to explore the unknown and new conditions with a focus that comes from being outside of an urban context—sometimes at the risk of formal incompletion." Karen Van Lengen

Attendees deliberated on the merit of repurposing and restoration of Roman monuments. Their votes, signatures, and an accompanying manifesto included here.

Being provincial meant being away from the center. For Jacque it was Manhattan, a specific intersection probably. Away from the center, you're at the edge. The power of looking from the edge is the ability to discover weakness and possibilities at the center. A strength of this place has been its ability to capitalize on this. I have many friends teaching or working at the center (of course there is a bit of hubris here) who are so worried about making sure they're doing "centric" things, the right kind of things, that they could be paralyzed. Whereas down here we know we're so out of it, no one is going to know what we're doing really, until it's too late. And then typically it turns out that what has been underway is the beginning of something new and important. The other day, I was looking at a course I taught in the late seventies called "Architecture as Landscape"—this at time when landscape was more a problem for building than anything else. The Lawn, Monticello, the James River plantations were something new to me and revealed a way to build with nature that was critical to my development. This would have never happened at the center! When I interviewed here at the end of the sixties it was quite a revelation. While other schools I was visiting were in disarray due to the social unraveling of the time and the extreme displeasure in the current war adventure, Virginia remained committed to architecture. To impress me with the social-ethical nature of the place, I was told how students had given up wearing sports jackets for a day in a vivid display of anarchy. But what so impressed was how during such a troubled time, so many thought that architecture mattered. I think that attitude remains strong.

KVL How did you come into our program? I am interested to know as a student what you thought about it? Obviously it's a lot more different than what you thought it would be when you came in. How did that play out for you?

MP I feel like my background was very formally driven. I just threw that out the window for a little while to open myself up to all the interesting stuff that was going on, which in a lot of cases had nothing to do inherently with architecture, but it was maybe dealing with how architecture might respond to these other things that are going on, whether they're socially driven, or environmentally charged, which I found really refreshing. The question then is what is it that drives us? And I think that's what we struggled with in this process... you talk about the Lawn being messy and the structure of the School being similar and it's true we're all overlapping. but there is an agenda.

KVL When I first came as dean, I went to visit all the other deans to introduce myself and every one of them talked about their Schools in relation to Jefferson. I was overwhelmed by the thought that this Founding Father loomed so large in the lives of everyone. I'd taught at the University of Pennsylvania and Ben Franklin is not at the center of every conversation. And he was not an unimportant historical figure. Of course Jefferson looms large because of the architecture—the values of the architecture inform all of the disciplines here—and that is the power of architecture. And I thought, "I can live with that. That's a lot to work with!"

RH Could you pinpoint various external events to help us frame things that have helped shape the school?

GAA We've been trying to map out a series of events in recent years that have shaped our contemporary reality, as a way to help us frame our work. We started in the nineties with various economic and environmental events: the dot-com bubble, 9/11, Katrina, the global economic crisis, and most recently Sandy.

RD When does this map start? The nineties? That's the immediate present! You have to really rethink this. Think of the books that came out in the sixties: Banham's *Theory and Design in the First Machine Age*, Norberg-Schulz's *Intentions in Architecture*, or Venturi's *Complexity and Contradiction*. These represented a profound shift from the pragmatics of the fifties to a mode of theoretical thinking that has sustained most discourse ever since. The economic slowdown of the seventies was absolutely critical, because that was when some of the most interesting formal advances in architecture were shaped because no one was building. So that economic crisis produced a body of theory that drove thinking for a long time.

In a very different way Katrina has played a crucial role here. When Karen announced to the faculty that of course as a School we would have to deal with the implications of this event, the shock was palpable and yet the ideas and work that came out of that period changed the culture of the School.

No longer was heroic resistance to natural crises a reasonable response. Accepting that we were sharing the planet with a force of nature that was not that concerned with human desire required a substantial shift in thinking and changed the way many considered landscapes and constructed works.

RM What do you think is the thread that holds together the discipline, the academy, and in particular our School? And what is the significance of this moment and this place?

KVL The thread is the struggle to reshape and grow our democratic culture, the working together of people toward some sense of purpose and equality.

"We're talking about a much longer cycle. One has to think about a potentially dystopian future—and not romantically. What would we do, if given the opportunity? And if that were to be done, how could that be a kind of stimulus, or catalyst to better thinking, better practice? That's both naive and hopeful. I think once you stop being optimistic, and become cynical, then it's all over. Architecture has to be an optimistic undertaking." Robin Dripps

There are great challenges in today's culture and its current economic hierarchies. Starting with large heroic ideas may be difficult. Smaller incremental moves from diverse and multiple perspectives seem more promising. In order to do that it requires innovative thinking, patience, and a great deal of perspective. I talked earlier about the role of the architect as one who orchestrates, or in our discipline of design and making one who creates any act of environmental transformation. This is a process of orchestrating change. The ethic of our work is in understanding the consequences of design decisions. And the challenge in experimental work is to do enough research to make informed decisions as we experiment and then to have the courage to revisit the effectiveness of those ideas as we move forward.

RD I like to think of work as a catalyst, a starting point, not a conclusion. Sometimes a small action, a small work, something incomplete and fragmentary has the ability to initiate further action with the hope that the accumulation of these pieces makes a substantial contribution. Sadly, architects are not always called upon to do important work. Commissions can be banal.

And yet these often have the potential to do more than was asked.

The other thing that keeps me going is the thing that we're all staring at. The environment is changing. And in a very problematic way and in a very rapid way. We are in denial. I was actually hoping for a little more disaster, in some of these events—not being cynical—but, I think it's the only thing that is going to make people react. So I'm thinking, OK, let's think of the worst. What would we do? What would we be prepared to do? Because at that point, we don't want to say, "Oh my God, we're in trouble here. What are we going to do?" It would be irresponsible to not have thought about this in advance, and not to have directed teaching towards answers.

KVL I think that is a very good point: one has to be able to imagine something so catastrophic that it requires our very best thinking and making to address this. Hopefully we are developing processes and programs here that support this perspective.

GAA We've spent a good amount of time thinking how the environmental conditions, be it climate or political environments, become catalysts that shape new modes of practice and pedagogy, and basically really shape our response. But how does our response then in turn reshape some of these forces that make up our contemporary reality? This really has been our challenge. Perhaps this is a litmus test for the agency of design in reshaping the environment. Even if we are only imagining the change, the cycle, the feedback loop, what is that loop? Is there really reciprocity? Do they really shape and reshape each other?

RD I think so, but it's a very slow feedback cycle. That's the difficulty. You want to see dramatic change but students are here for only two or three years.

GAA This is perhaps why it's great to be in the academy at the moment, to teach or to be a student, in this moment of crisis, because it actually allows you to imagine utopias or dystopias, prophecies or paradigm shifts, whereas in practice this is perhaps less relevant or possible.

RD Yes, this is why the academy is so important. This is why I am so vocal in my distress about teaching contract documents. This idea of "training," and I mean that literally for the profession, whereas I think we need to be training for a profession that we don't even know what is going to be.

"I like to think of work as a catalyst, a starting point, not a conclusion. Sometimes a small action, a small work, something incomplete and fragmentary has the ability to initiate further action with the hope that the accumulation of these pieces makes a substantial contribution." Robin Dripps

Lectures and Events

Exhibit: The India Initiative

Exhibit: Framing India
[Michael Petrus]

The Emerging Megacity and the Enduring Village
[Phoebe Crisman and Peter Waldman, India Initiative Symposium]

Carlo Scarpa's Brion Tomb and the Landscape of the Veneto
[Vitale Zanchettin, Veneto Society Visiting Lecture Series]

The "New Brutalism of Carlo Scarpa"
[Maddalena Scimemi, Veneto Society Visiting Lecture Series]

Venetian Building Traditions in Carlo Scarpa's Hands
[Vitale Zanchettin, Veneto Society Visiting Lecture Series]

Howland Memorial Lecture: Petrochemical America
[Kate Orff, SCAPE]

Exhibit: Beijing Urbanism
[Peking University / University of Virginia Design Workshop]

Exhibit: Sambo Reconfigured
[Mara Marcu, University of Virginia]

Exhibit: Beyond the Book: The Legacy of Rachel Carson and Silent Spring

Society of Architectural Historians Lecture
[Calder Loth]

Friday Talks: Community Advantage: Responding to Globalization
[Suzanne Moomaw, University of Virginia]

LUNCH 7 Release

31	31	14	17	21	22	24	28	28	28	10	12	12
August		September								October		

India Symposium:
Vikramditya Prakash + Tod Williams

Kate Orff

Vortex: All-School workshop

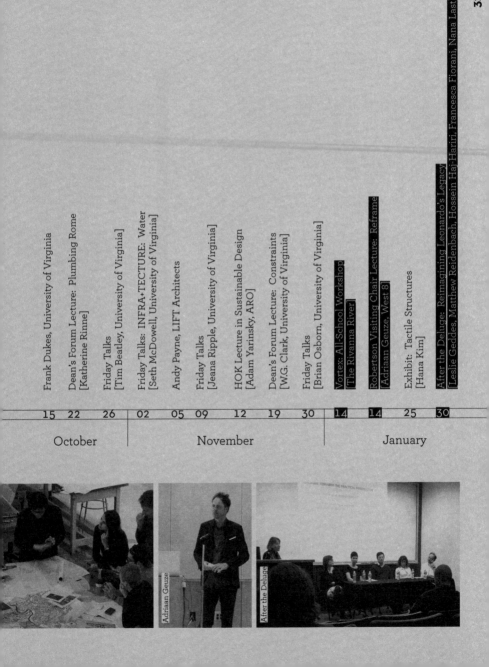

Frank Dukes, University of Virginia

Dean's Forum Lecture: Plumbing Rome
[Katherine Rinne]

Friday Talks
[Tim Beatley, University of Virginia]

Friday Talks: INFRA+TECTURE: Water
[Seth McDowell, University of Virginia]

Andy Payne, LIFT Architects

Friday Talks
[Jeana Ripple, University of Virginia]

HOK Lecture in Sustainable Design
[Adam Yarinsky, ARO]

Dean's Forum Lecture: Constraints
[W.G. Clark, University of Virginia]

Friday Talks
[Brian Osborn, University of Virginia]

Vortex: All-School Workshop
[The Rivanna River]

Robertson Visiting Chair Lecture: Reframe
[Adriaan Geuze, West 8]

Exhibit: Tactile Structures
[Hana Kim]

After the Deluge: Reimagining Leonardo's Legacy
[Leslie Geddes, Matthew Reidenbach, Hossein Haj-Hariri, Francesca Fiorani, Nana Last]

| 15 | 22 | 26 | 02 | 05 | 09 | 12 | 19 | 30 | 14 | 14 | 25 | 30 |

October · November · January

Adriaan Geuze

After the Deluge

Dean's Forum Lecture
[Ramon Prat, ACTAR Publishers]

Michael Owen Jones Lecture
[Matthias Hollwich, Hollwich Kushner (HWKN)]

Woltz Symposium

Carlo Pelliccia Travelling Fellowship Exhibition
[Teppei Iizuka, Kirsten Sparenborg]

Sarah McArthur Nix Travelling Fellowship Exhibition
[Alan Ford, Matthew Pinyan, Parker Sutton]

Exhibit: Biennale Box - W.G. Clark's Collection

After the Deluge: The Rising
[Matthew Burtner, Iñaki Alday, Leena Cho, Matthew Jull,
Patricia Wiberg]

Clark-Howe Colloquium: City Center DC
[Matt O'Malley, Armstrong Yakubu, Robert Sponseller]

Towers and Caverns
[Iñaki Abalos and Renata Sentkiewicz, Abalos+Sentkiewicz arquitectos]

Thaler Memorial Lecture
[Warren Byrd, Nelson Byrd Woltz]

Clark-Howe Colloquium: The Essential and Necessary
[Kevin Gannon, Architecture for Humanity]

Clark-Howe Colloquium: Linking Water with Development in the 21st Century
[Vincent Lee, ARUP]

01	04	09	10	10	12	20	21	25	04	11	19

February   March

All-School Workshop

Painting the American Flag

Adriaan Geuze

After the Deluge: The Contaminated
[Brandon Ballengée, Phoebe Crisman, Jim Smith, Lydia Moyer, Rebecca Dillingham]

Thaler Memorial Lecture
[Thomas Woltz, Nelson Byrd Woltz]

Clark-Howe Colloquium: Hands-on Design
[Aleksey Lukyanov-Cherny, SITU STUDIO|SITU FABRICATION]

After the Deluge: The Disappearing
[Margaret Ross Tolbert, Brian Richter, Paolo D'Odorico, Janet Herman]

INTENSITIES
[Marc Tsurmaki, Lewis.Tsurmaki.Lewis]

The Networked Environment of Lighting
[Linnaea Tillett, Tillett Lighting Design]

Negro Building: Black Americans in the World of Fairs and Museums
[Mabel Wilson, Columbia University]

Thomas Jefferson Foundation Medalist
[Laurie Olin]

Landscapes of Post-Modernity
[Sonia Hirt, Virginia Tech]

Stan Winston Arts Festival of the Moving Creature

Exhibit: Painting the American Flag and Works on Paper
[Sanda Iliescu and Painting & Public Ar (ARCH 5780)]

Benjamin Howland Fellowship - Expanding Eruv
[Isaac Cohen, Isaac Hametz, Rae Vassar]

| 20 | 25 | 28 | 29 | 01 | 05 | 08 | 12 | 19 | 20 | 26 | 26 |

March | April

Marc Tsurmaki

Laurie Olin

Spring 2013 Final Reviews

Final Reviews

Fall 2012 - Undergraduate Reviews Guest Jurors
Michelle Addington, Yale School of Architecture
Sho-Ping Chin, Payette Associates
Andrew Cocke, Catholic University School of Architecture and Planning
Grace La, Harvard Graduate School of Design
Paul King, EYP Architecture & Engineering
Fernando Rodrigues, HOK
Jason Young, Taubman College of Architecture and Urban Planning

Fall 2012 - Graduate Reviews Guest Jurors
Beata Corcoran, Vergason Landscape architects
Mark Klopfer, Wentworth Institute of Technology
Jonathan Massey, Syracuse University School of Architecture
Marc Miller, Cornell University AAP
Carmen Trudell, Cal Poly Architecture
Sylvia Smith, FXFowle Architects
Mabel Wilson, Columbia University Graduate School of Architecture, Planning and Preservation

Spring 2012 - Graduate Reviews Guest Jurors
Tom Bishop, BRB Architects
Carrie Burke, Parabola Architecture
Kevin Burke, Parabola Architecture

Michael Cadwell, Knowlton School of Architecture
Brad Cantrell, LSU School of Architecture
Yolande Daniels, studioSUMO
Lluis Domenech, BSAV Barcelona
Frank Harmon, F Harmon Architect
Jane Hutton, Harvard Graduate School of Design
Carlos Jimenez, Rice School of Architecture
Brian Katen, Virginia Tech College of Architecture and Urban Studies
Star Keene, SHoP Architects
Audrey Matlock, A Matlock Architects
Eugene Ryang, Waterstreetstudio

Spring 2012 - Undergraduate Reviews Guest Jurors
Governor Baliles, University of Virginia Miller Center of Public Affairs
Eric Gartner, SPG Architects
Sally Gilliland, Hudson Inc
Margaret Griffin, SCI-Arc
Lisa Iwamoto, UC Berkeley College of Environmental Design
Olle Lundberg, Lundberg Design
Matthew Slaats, The Bridge
Nader Tehrani, MIT School of Architecture and Planning
Joy Wang, RUR Architecture

SCHOOL OF ARCHITECTURE ADMINISTRATION

Kim Tanzer
Dean and Edward E. Elson Professor of Architecture

Iñaki Alday
Chair, Dept of Architecture || Quesada Professor

Timothy Beatley
Chair, Dept of Urban & Environmental Planning || Heinz Professor of Sustainable Communities

Nancy A. Takahashi
Chair, Dept of Landscape Architecture || Distinguished Lecturer

Richard Guy Wilson
Chair, Dept of Architectural History || Commonwealth Professor

Phoebe Crisman
Associate Dean for Research || Director of Global Sustainability Minor || Associate Professor

Allen Lee
Associate Dean for Finance & Administration

Kirk Martini
Associate Dean for Academics || Associate Professor

John Quale
Director of Graduate Architecture Program || Associate Professor

Betsy Roettger
Director of Undergraduate Architecture Program || Lecturer

Daniel Bluestone
Director of Historic Preservation Program || Professor

DEPARTMENT OF ARCHITECTURE

Iñaki Alday Quesada Professor || Chair

W.G. Clark Edmund Schureman Campbell Professor

Robin Dripps T. David Fitz-Gibbon Professor

Edward Ford Vincent and Eleanor Shea Professor

Shiqiao Li Weedon Professor of Architecture

Karen Van Lengen William R. Kenan, Jr. Professor

Peter Waldman William R. Kenan, Jr. Professor

Manuel Bailo Associate Professor

Anselmo Canfora Associate Professor

Phoebe Crisman Associate Professor || Director of Global Sustainability Minor

Sanda Iliescu Associate Professor

Nana Last Associate Professor

Earl Mark Associate Professor

Kirk Martini Associate Professor || Associate Dean for Academics

Charlie Menefee Associate Professor

John Quale Associate Professor || Director of Graduate Architecture Program

Bill Sherman Professor || Associate Vice President for Research

Matthew Jull Assistant Professor

Seth McDowell Assistant Professor

Jeana Ripple Assistant Professor

Ghazal Abbasy-Asbagh Lecturer

C. Pamela Black Lecturer

Margarita Jover Lecturer

Alexander Kitchin Lecturer

Esther Lorenz Lecturer

Mara Marcu Lecturer || Virginia Teaching Fellow

Leslie McDonald Lecturer

Karolin Moellmann Lecturer

Gwenedd Murray Lecturer

Jordi Nebot Lecturer

Lucia Phinney Distinguished Lecturer

Betsy Roettger Lecturer || Director of Undergraduate Architecture Program

Schaeffer Somers Lecturer

Charles Sparkman Lecturer

Lester Yuen Lecturer

DEPARTMENT OF ARCHITECTURAL HISTORY

Daniel Bluestone Professor || Director of Historic Preservation Program

Richard Guy Wilson Commonwealth Professor || Chair

Cammy Brothers Associate Professor || Valmarana Professor

Shiqiao Li Weedon Professor of Architecture

Sheila Crane Associate Professor

Yunsheng Huang Associate Professor

Louis Nelson Associate Professor

Lisa Reilly Associate Professor

Fraser D. Neiman Lecturer

DEPARTMENT OF LANDSCAPE ARCHITECTURE

Reuben M. Rainey William Stone Weedon Professor Emeritus

Elizabeth Meyer Professor

Julie Bargmann Associate Professor

Teresa Gali-Izard Associate Professor

Michael Lee Reuben M. Rainey Professor in the History of Landscape Architecture

Jorg Sieweke Assistant Professor

C. Cole Burrell Lecturer

Leena Cho Lecturer

Chloe Hawkins Lecturer

Rob McGinnis Lecturer

Brian Osborn Lecturer || Virginia Teaching Fellow

Peter O'Shea Lecturer

Adalie Pierce-McManamon Lecturer

Lauren Sasso Lecturer

Nancy A. Takahashi Distinguished Lecturer || Chair

Mary Warinner Lecturer

DEAN'S OFFICE

Cynthia Smith Assistant to the Dean

Seth Wood Communications Coordinator

Cally Bryant Graphic Designer

ADMINISTRATIVE SUPPORT

Adela Su Administrative Services Coordinator

Patty DeCourcy Administrative Assistant

Tim Kelley Assistant to the Chair

STUDENT SERVICES

Sharon McDonald Director of Student Records and Registration

Kristine Nelson Director of Admissions and Financial Aid

Cypress Walker Student Services Coordinator

FINANCIAL AND HUMAN RESOURCES

Lisa Benton Business Manager

Leslie Fitzgerald Business Officer

Kathy Woodson Human Resources Coordinator

COMPUTING AND INFORMATION TECHNOLOGY

Jake Thackston Systems Manager, Systems Engineer

Eric M. Field Director of the Insight Lab, Applied & Advanced Technology

Dav Banks Webmaster, Systems Engineer

Tony Horning Classroom Support

Terrance Sheltra Labs & Studios

John Vigour Student & Faculty Support

FACILITIES

Melissa Goldman Fabrication Facilities Manager

Dick Smith Facilities Manager

INSTITUTE FOR ENVIRONMENTAL NEGOTIATIONS

Frank Dukes Director

Tanya Denckla Cobb Associate Director

Melissa Keywood Program Manager, VA Natural Resources Leadership Institute

Ellen J. Martin Supervisory Grants and Office Manager

Tammy Switzer Administrative Assistant

SCHOOL OF ARCHITECTURE FOUNDATION

Warren Buford Executive Director

Kimberly Wong Haggart Associate Director of Alumni Relations   Donna Rose Office Manager

June Yang Associate Director of Development

Acknowledgements

Iñaki Alday, Cally Bryant, W.G. Clark, Rebecca Cooper, Sheila Crane, Ricardo Devesa, Robin Dripps, Jason Eversman, Eric Field, Jake Fox, Teresa Gali-Izard, Sanda Iliescu, Margarita Jover, Nana Last, Allen Lee, Mara Marcu, Lucia Phinney, Ramon Prat, John Quale, Ingeborg Rocker, Betsy Roettger, Bill Sherman, Cynthia Smith, Dick Smith, Scott Smith, Charles Sparkman, Megan Suau, Nancy Takahashi, Kim Tanzer, Karen Van Lengen, Peter Waldman, Seth Wood

CATALYST EDITORIAL TEAM

Editor
Ghazal Abbasy-Asbagh, Lecturer in Architecture

Student Editorial Team
Rebecca Hora, M.Arch 2013
Ryan Metcalf, M.Arch 2013
Matthew Pinyan, M.Arch 2013

ADVISORY COUNCIL
Iñaki Alday
Timothy Beatley
Sheila Crane
Robin Dripps
Teresa Gali-Izard
Nana Last
Nancy Takahashi
Kim Tanzer

GRAPHIC DESIGN
Actar Publishers
Paper Matters

Printed in Grafos S.A.

COPY EDITOR
Jason Eversman

PHOTO CREDITS
Model photos - Scott Smith
Installations - Jake Fox
Events - Cally Bryant and Paper Matters

PAPER MATTERS 2012-2013
Ghazal Abbasy-Asbagh (Lecturer), Iñaki Alday
(Quesada Professor and Chair, Department of
Architecture), Danielle Alexander (MLA '14),
Rebecca Cooper (Fine Arts Architecture and
Instruction Librarian), Robin Dripps (T. David
Fitz-Gibbon Professor of Architecture), Phoebe
Harris (B.S.Arch '13), Rebecca Hora (M.Arch
'13), Carlos Jennings (B.S.Arch '13), Nick Knodt
(M.Arch '14), Ryan Metcalf (M.Arch '13), Matt
Pinyan (M.Arch '13), Mariam Ramatullah (B.S.Arch
'13), Charles Sparkman (Lecturer, M.Arch '12),
Clayton Williams (M.Arch '14)

Distribution
Actar D
151 Grand Street, 5th floor
New York, NY 10013, USA
T +1 212 966 2207
F +1 212 966 2214
salesnewyork@actar-d.com

ISBN: 978-1-940291-00-0

Catalyst **is a joint production
of Paper Matters and Actar D.**